Too Late to Awaken

Too Late to Awaken

What Lies Ahead When There is No Future?

SLAVOJ ŽIŽEK

ALLEN LANE
an imprint of
PENGUIN BOOKS

ALLEN LANE

UK | USA | Canada | Ireland | Australia
India | New Zealand | South Africa

Allen Lane is part of the Penguin Random House group of companies
whose addresses can be found at global.penguinrandomhouse.com

Penguin
Random House
UK

First published 2023
001

Copyright © Slavoj Žižek, 2023

The moral right of the author has been asserted

Set in 12/14.75pt Dante MT Std
Typeset by Jouve (UK), Milton Keynes
Printed and bound in Great Britain by Clays Ltd, Elcograf S.p.A.

The authorized representative in the EEA is Penguin Random House Ireland,
Morrison Chambers, 32 Nassau Street, Dublin D02 YH68

A CIP catalogue record for this book is available from the British Library

ISBN: 978–0–241–65175–9

www.greenpenguin.co.uk

MIX
Paper | Supporting
responsible forestry
FSC
www.fsc.org   FSC® C018179

Penguin Random House is committed to a
sustainable future for our business, our readers
and our planet. This book is made from Forest
Stewardship Council® certified paper.

Contents

Introduction: Between *Futur and* Avenir

As an obsessional neurotic, I regularly wake up a couple of minutes before my alarm clock rings, no matter what time I set it for and no matter what time zone I'm in. But it would be wrong to read this idiosyncrasy as a sign that I'm fully aware of the need to wake up: it's more that I do it to avoid the traumatic experience of being woken. Why?

The apostle Paul characterized his own time in a way that seems to fit our present moment perfectly: 'Make no mistake about the age we live in; already it is high time for us to awake out of our sleep'(Romans 13:11). However, recent historical experience rather seems to demonstrate the opposite: *there is no right moment to awaken.* We either freak out too early and thus appear to spread empty panic, or we come to our senses when it's already too late. We solace ourselves with the thought that there is still time to act, and then, all of a sudden, we realize that there isn't. Again: why?

When somebody stays up working or amusing himself into the small hours, we usually tell him it's too late to be awake. But what if, in our historical moment, it's rather too late to awaken? We hear all the time that it's five minutes (or one minute, or even ten seconds) to noon, to global doomsday, so now is our last chance to avert disaster. But what if the only way to prevent a catastrophe is to assume that it has already happened – that we're already five minutes past zero hour?

So what lies ahead when there is no future? In French (and some other languages, like my own, Slovene), there are two

1

words for 'future' that in English cannot be adequately differentiated: *futur* and *avenir*. *Futur* stands for the future as the continuation of the present: the full actualization of tendencies that are already in place. *Avenir* points towards a radical break, a discontinuity with the present – to something new that is to come (*à venir*), not just what will be. If Trump had won against Biden in the 2020 elections, he would have been (before the elections) the future president, but not the president to come.

In today's apocalyptic situation, our ultimate horizon – the *futur* – is what Jean-Pierre Dupuy calls the dystopian 'fixed point': a zero-point of nuclear war, ecological breakdown, global economic and social chaos, Russia's attack on Ukraine exploding into a new world war, and so on. Even if it is indefinitely postponed, this zero-point is the 'attractor' towards which our reality, left to itself, will tend. The way to combat this future catastrophe is through acts that interrupt our drift towards the 'fixed point'. We can see here how ambiguous the Sex Pistols' 'no future' chant really is: at a deeper level, it designates not the impossibility of change but precisely what we should be striving for – to break the hold that the catastrophic 'future' has over us, and thereby to open up a space for something New 'to come'.

Dupuy's meaning is that, if we are to confront properly the threat of catastrophe, we have to introduce a new notion of time, the 'time of a project'. We should conceive of a closed circuit between the past and the future: the future is causally produced by our acts in the past, while the way that we act is determined by our anticipation of the future, and our reaction to what we have anticipated. If we perceive catastrophe as our fate, as unavoidable, and then project ourselves into that future, adopting its standpoint, we will retroactively insert into its past (the past of the future) counterfactual possibilities ('If we were to do that and that, this catastrophe wouldn't have occurred!'). We can then act upon those possibilities today.[1]

Is this not what Adorno and Horkheimer sought to do with their 'dialectic of Enlightenment'? While traditional Marxism enjoined us to act in order to bring about a Communist future, Adorno and Horkheimer projected themselves into a catastrophic future (the advent of the 'administered society', the *verwaltete Welt*, of total technological manipulation) in order to make us act to avoid it. And, ironically, doesn't the same hold for the defeat of the Soviet Union? It's easy, from today's perspective, to mock the 'pessimists', from the Right to the Left, from Solzhenitsyn to Castoriadis, who deplored the blindness and compromises of the democratic West, its lack of ethico-political strength and courage in dealing with the Communist threat, and who predicted that the West had already lost the Cold War, that the Communist bloc had already won it, that the collapse of the West was imminent – but in fact it was precisely their attitude that did the most to bring about the collapse of Communism. In Dupuy's terms, it was their very 'pessimistic' prediction of the future, of how history would inevitably unfold, that mobilized them to counteract it.

We should thus invert the commonplace according to which we perceive the present as full of possibilities and ourselves as agents free to choose among them, while, in retrospect, our choices appear to us as fully determined and necessary. It is, on the contrary, the engaged agents of the present who perceive themselves as caught in Destiny, while, from the standpoint of later observation, we can discern alternatives in the past, the possibility of events taking another path.

To put it another way, the past is open to retroactive reinterpretation, while the future is closed. This doesn't mean that we cannot change the future; it just means that, in order to do so, we should first (not 'understand' but) change our past, reinterpreting it in such a way that it opens up towards a different future. Will the Russian attack on Ukraine trigger a new world war? The answer can only be a paradoxical one: if there is a new war, it will be a necessary one. Dupuy says: 'if an outstanding event takes place, a catastrophe, for example, it could not not have taken place; nonetheless, insofar as it did not take place, it is not inevitable. It is thus the event's actualization – the fact that it takes place – which retroactively creates its necessity.'[2] Once a full military conflict has broken out (between the US and Iran, between China and Taiwan, between Russia and NATO . . .), it will appear to us all as necessary; that is to say, we will automatically read the past that led to it as a sequence of events that necessarily caused the explosion. If it doesn't happen, we will read it the way we read the Cold War today: as a series of dangerous moments where catastrophe was avoided because both sides were aware of the deadly consequences of a global conflict.

There is a story (almost certainly apocryphal) about Zhou Enlai, the Chinese Prime Minister. It goes like this: when, in 1953, he was in Geneva for the peace negotiations to end the Korean war, a French journalist asked him what he thought about the French Revolution. Zhou replied: 'It is too early to tell.' In a way, he was right. With the disintegration of the East European 'people's democracies' in the late 1990s, the struggle for the historical place of the French Revolution flared up again. Liberal revisionists argued that the demise of Communism in 1989 occurred at exactly the right moment, marking the end of an era that began in 1789 – it was, they held, the final failure of the revolutionary model that first entered the scene with the Jacobins. But the battle for the French Revolution goes on today: if a new space of radical emancipatory politics emerges, then the Revolution will no longer appear to be a historical dead end. But back to Zhou: it now seems that what most probably really happened is as follows. In 1972, when Henry Kissinger visited China, he asked Zhou what he thought about the 1968 rebellion in France – and it was to this question that Zhou gave the answer, 'It is too early to tell.' And he was right again: 1968 was a Leftist anti-establishment rebellion, but its slogans (against 'alienated' university education, for sexual freedom, and so on) were soon appropriated by the establishment and enabled the smooth passage to neoliberal permissive capitalism; university education superseded by quick management courses, sexual liberation ending up in commodification of sexuality. It is in this sense that

> insofar as the future is not rendered present, one has to think of it as simultaneously inclusive of the catastrophic event and of its not-taking-place – not as disjunctive possibilities but as a conjunction of states one or the other of which will reveal itself *a posteriori* as necessary the moment the present chooses it.[3]

It is not that we have two possibilities: either military, ecological and social catastrophe, or recovery. This formula is all too easy. What we have are two *superposed necessities*.[4] In our predicament, it is both necessary that there will be a global catastrophe and that all contemporary history moves towards it, *and* necessary that we act to prevent it. When these two superposed necessities collapse, only one of them will come into being, so in either case our history will (have) be(en) necessary.

From my youth in socialist Yugoslavia, I remember a weird incident with toilet paper. All of a sudden, a rumour started to circulate that there wasn't enough toilet paper in the shops. The authorities promptly issued assurances that there was enough toilet paper to meet normal demand, and, surprisingly, not only was this true but people mostly believed it was true. However, the average consumer reasoned in the following way: I know that there is enough toilet paper and that the rumour is false, but what if some people take it seriously and, in a panic, start buying up excessive reserves of toilet paper, and in so doing cause an actual shortage? I'd better buy some reserves myself . . . It was not even necessary for this customer to believe that other shoppers took the rumour seriously – it was enough for them to presuppose that there were others who believed that there were others who believed it. The effect was the same, namely, a real lack of toilet paper in the shops. This behaviour should not be confused with the stance we have to adopt today – with our need to accept the inevitability of catastrophe: in contrast to the rumour, which began as a lie but then gave rise to the reality to which it referred, our world is effectively sliding towards catastrophe, and our problem is not that of the self-fulfilling prophecy, but rather of self-sabotage – we keep talking about the threat in order to do nothing.

No wonder, then, that some researchers are now suggesting a new answer to the big question: if intelligent extraterrestrials have already visited Earth, why didn't they try to establish contact with us humans?[5] The answer: what if they observed us closely for some time but did not find us of any particular interest? We are the dominant species on a relatively small planet propelling its civilization towards multiple kinds of self-destruction (climate and ecological breakdown, nuclear self-annihilation, global social unrest), while doing nothing much about it. That's not even to mention local stupidities like

today's Politically Correct liberal 'Left' which, instead of working for a large social solidarity, subjects even its potential allies
to pseudo-moral purist admission criteria, seeing sexism and
racism everywhere and thus making new enemies everywhere.[6] Take, for instance, the response to Bernie Sanders'
warning that the Democrats should focus not only on abortion
rights ahead of the midterm elections in November 2022. He
argued that the Democrats needed to embrace a broad agenda
that also addressed the economic woes facing America,
countering 'anti-worker' views from Republicans and the ways
that their policies could hurt the working class.[7] Although
Sanders has a 100 per cent pro-choice voting record, die-hard
liberal feminists immediately counterattacked, accusing him
of anti-feminism. The same aliens would notice a no less
strange fact from the opposite side of the political spectrum: in
her short time as British prime minister, Liz Truss's economic
policy followed what she perceived as the demands of the
market, ignoring working-class pleas for support. What led to
her downfall, however, was not popular discontent but rather
the fact that those same market forces (the stock exchange, big
corporations . . .) reacted with panic to her proposed budget.
Further proof, if it were needed, that today's politics represents
the interests of capital – no matter how progressive or populist
you are.

According to some media reports (denied by the Kremlin, as
expected), at the beginning of December 2022 Putin fell on the
stairs of his house and soiled himself[8] – the same thing that
happened to Biden when he visited the Pope in 2021.[9] Even if
these two anecdotes are apocryphal, *se non e vero e ben trovato*:
they provide a perfect metaphor of where we are today –
between the two shits, the new fundamentalist Right and the
liberal establishment Woke Left. Shit really is the order of the

day, incidentally: 'kopi luwak' is the world's most expensive coffee, and it's literally made from coffee beans that have been partially digested and then pooped out by the civet, a cat-like creature that lives in south-east Asia and sub-Saharan Africa. The civet's digestive enzymes change the structure of proteins in the coffee beans, which removes some of the acidity to make a smoother cup of coffee. It is mostly produced in Indonesia, and sells to customers in the US, where a cup of kopi luwak can cost up to $80.[10] Is today's prevailing ideology, particularly on the populist Right, not precisely a kind of ideological kopi luwak?

Some of the noblest parts of our emancipatory tradition (anti-Fascist and anti-racist struggle, rejection of our commercialized and hedonistic way of life, the fight against financial elites exploiting ordinary people, the efforts to abolish leftovers of colonization . . .) are being gulped down by political leaders around the world. Their neo-Fascist or neoliberal digestive enzymes are removing the radical acidity of the ideas they've swallowed, and turning them into pieces of shit that smoothly fit the existing global capitalist system, although they present themselves as its destruction.

Here we begin to touch on the delicate topic of the relationship between truth and lies. The following rather boring joke nonetheless concludes with an interesting final spin that does something to indicate the fix we're in. A wife asks her husband to run to a nearby shop to buy her a packet of cigarettes. He goes there, but, since it is already late in the evening, the shop is closed, so he goes to a bar instead. He gets into a flirtatious conversation with the voluptuous young woman behind the bar, and they end up in bed in her apartment. After a couple of hours of passionate lovemaking, he begins to worry how he will explain his long absence to his wife. Then he gets an idea – he asks the woman if she has some baby powder, and he rubs it into his hands. When he arrives home, his wife is furiously awaiting him and asks where he has been. He replies: 'The shop had already closed, so I went to a nearby bar to get the cigarettes. I began flirting with a voluptuous young woman who was serving at the bar, and we ended up in bed in her apartment. After a couple of hours of passionate lovemaking, I finally returned home . . .'

'You dirty liar!' interrupts his wife. 'You think I didn't notice the powder on your hands! You did what you'd been wanting to do for ages, even though I'd prohibited it – you went out for a late-night bowling session with your friends!'

This is how ideology functions today: ideology tells the truth but creates conditions which guarantee that the truth itself will be perceived as a lie. Take this example: in July 2022, the Belarussian president Alexander Lukashenko urged 'forgetful Europe' to go through a moral cleansing for the (Fascist) sins of its grandfathers and fathers;[11] however, the actual intention of this call was precisely to eliminate the radical, emancipatory, anti-Fascist tradition that forms the core of Europe. Such calls for moral cleansing tend to come in the run-up to undistilled outbursts of pure destructive rage. As Peter Sloterdijk pointed out, at the beginning of European civilization there was Homer's *Iliad,* which opens with the line on Achilles' wrath. Will, then, the first line of a poem about Europe's end be: 'Sing the rage of the President Putin, murderous, doomed, that cost the Europeans countless losses'? This rage was performed at a big gathering in the Red Square in October 2022, convened to celebrate the annexation of parts of Ukraine. The actor and singer Ivan Okhlobystin gave an inflammatory speech that ended with the following exhortation:

We should call it a Holy War! Holy War! There is an ancient
word in Russian: Goida. Goida is a call to immediate action. We
need a war cry like that today! Goida, brothers and sisters! Goida!
Fear us, people of the old world! Devoid of beauty, devoid of
faith, devoid of wisdom! A world run by madmen, perverts and
Satanists! Fear us – WE ARE COMING! GOIDA!!![12]

'Goida' means, especially today: 'Let's go! Don't think, just obey
and do it!' It is not just an ancient Russian word but one that was
a battle cry of the *oprichniki*, the private army of Ivan the
Terrible known for terrorizing his (real and imagined) enemies,
so it clearly implies ruthless terror, torture and killing. Incidentally, the only speech from recent history similar in tone to
Okhlobystin's is the infamous 'total war' speech made by Goeb-
bels in Berlin in early 1943, after the Stalingrad defeat. (Indeed, a
world of madmen, perverts and Satanists devoid of beauty, faith
and wisdom is quite an apposite description of Putin's world.)
We should note, though, that the Red Square celebration was a
fake event: the crowd was mostly composed of state officials
bussed in for the occasion, and most of them reacted to
Okhlobystin's speech with no enthusiasm, just indifference and
fear (applause and cheers were added later by the TV studio).

Although today's Russia is arguably the purest case of ideological kupi luwak, we should avoid the fateful trap of
constraining it to Russia and its allies. Are the Trumpian neo-
cons not offering a similar version of kupi luwak? And has the
noblest liberal-democratic ideology not also been processed by
our civets to legitimize global capitalist exploitation and
'humanitarian' military interventions? We are all in this shit,
not only up to our knees but – if I am allowed to use a tasteless
metaphor – up to our arses.

So those aliens would, for sure, come to the conclusion that it is much safer to simply ignore us in order not to be contaminated with our disease. On the other hand, if we were to choose *something new* to come – then, maybe, we'd deserve their attention. The present book looks for clues that show how we might do that. It urgently tries to contribute to a true awakening – one that is more than merely a sobering recognition of how things really are. Even more than that, we need an awakening to what we are not yet, and could still become.

Goodbye Lenin, Welcome to Impotent Aggressors

To paraphrase the well-known title of one of Freud's essays, we can observe today the universal tendency of debasement in the sphere of public life. At a press conference held a fortnight before the Russian invasion of Ukraine, Vladimir Putin noted that the Ukrainian government did not like the Minsk Agreement, which, in seeking to end the Donbas war, granted the region temporary self-governance. He added: 'Like it or not, it's your duty, my beauty.' The saying has well-known sexual connotations: Putin appeared to be quoting from 'Sleeping Beauty in a Coffin' by the Soviet-era punk rock group Red Mold: 'Sleeping beauty in a coffin, I crept up and fucked her. Like it, or dislike it, sleep my beauty.'[13] Although the Kremlin press representative claimed that Putin was using an old folkloric expression, its coarse casting of Ukraine as an object of necrophilia and rape was clear. Putin has form: twenty years earlier, he replied to a question from a Western journalist with a vulgar threat of castration: 'If you want to become a complete Islamic radical and are ready to undergo circumcision, then I invite you to Moscow. We are a multidenominational country. We have specialists in this question [circumcision]. I will recommend that they carry out the operation in such a way so that afterward, nothing else will grow.'[14] No wonder, then, that Putin and Trump were buddies in vulgarity. The counter-argument you often hear at this point is that at least politicians like Putin and Trump openly say what they mean, and avoid hypocrisy. Here, however, I am wholeheartedly on the side of hypocrisy: the form (of hypocrisy) is never just a form, it compels us to make the content less brutal.

Putin's obscene remark should be read against the background of the Ukrainian crisis, which is presented in our media as the threat of the 'rape of a fair country'. This crisis is not without its comical aspects – proof, in today's topsy-turvy world, that the crisis is serious. A Slovene political analyst, Boris Čibej, pointed out the comical character of the tensions around Ukraine at the beginning of 2022: 'Those who are expected to attack [i.e. Russia] claim they have no intention of doing so, and those who act as if they want to calm the situation down insist that conflict is inevitable.'[15] We can go on here: the US, protector of Ukraine, warned that war could explode at any moment while the Ukrainian president warned against war hysteria and called for calm. It is easy to translate this situation into terms of sexual violence: Russia, which was ready to rape Ukraine, claimed it didn't want to do it – but between the lines mades it clear that, if it didn't get consent for sex from Ukraine, it was ready to get what it wanted by force (recall Putin's vulgar reply); on top of this, it accused Ukraine of provoking it. The US sounded the alarm about the imminent threat of rape so that it could assert itself as the protector of post-Soviet states – a protectiveness which cannot but remind us of a local mobster who offers stores and restaurants in his domain protection against robbery, with a veiled threat that, if they reject his protection, something may happen to them . . . Ukraine, the target of the threat, tried to keep calm, unnerved by the US alarm bells; aware, too, that the uproar about rape might push Russia to actually commit it.

Now, eighteen months into this brutal conflict, how can we make sense of it, of all its unpredictable dangers? What if this conflict is so dangerous not because it reflects the growing strength of the two ex-superpowers but, on the contrary, proves that they are not able to accept the fact that they are no longer true global powers? When, at the height of the Cold War, Mao Ze Dong said that the US was, despite all its weapons, a paper tiger, he forgot to add that paper tigers could be more dangerous than real ones. The fiasco of their withdrawal from Afghanistan was just the last in a series of blows to US geopolitical supremacy, while Russia's efforts to reconstruct the Soviet empire represent nothing but a desperate attempt to cover up the fact that it is now a weak, decaying state. As is also the case with actual rapists, rape ultimately signals the impotence of the aggressor.

This impotence became palpable with the first direct penetration of the Russian military into foreign territory – first, that is, if we discount the obscene role of the Wagner group, a private military company whose contractors took part in various earlier conflicts, including operations in Syria, Crimea, the Central African Repulic and the Republika Srpska in Bosnia. This group of anonymous mercenaries, once a remote unit of the Russian Ministry of Defence used by the Russian government in conflicts where deniability was required, operated for years in Donbas, organizing 'spontaneous' resistance to Ukrainian rule (as they already did in Crimea). When these tensions exploded into war, the Russian Duma passed a direct appeal to Putin to recognize the Russian-controlled separatist states of Donetsk and Luhansk. Putin at first said that he would not immediately recognize the so-called republics, meaning that when he did recognize them he appeared merely to be reacting to popular pressure from below. This tactic followed rules described and practised decades ago by Stalin. In the mid 1920s, Stalin proposed to simply proclaim that the government of the Russian Soviet Federated Socialist Republic was also the government of five surrounding republics (Ukraine, Belarus,

Azerbaijan, Armenia, Georgia). This executive decision should, he argued, be presented as the will of the people:

> If the present decision is confirmed by the Central Committee of the Russian Communist Party, it will not be made public, but communicated to the Central Committees of the Republics for circulation among the Soviet organs, the Central Executive Committees or the Congresses of the Soviets of the said Republics before the convocation of the All-Russian Congress of the Soviets, where it will be declared to be the wish of these Republics.[16]

The interaction of the higher authority (the Central Committee) with its base is thus not only abolished, so that the higher authority can simply impose its will; to add insult to injury, it is staged as its opposite. The Central Committee decides what the base will ask the higher authority to enact, as if it were its own wish. Recall the most conspicuous case of such staging, from 1939: having occupied the three Baltic states, the Soviet Union organized a 'referendum' in which states 'freely' asked to join the Soviet Union, which naturally granted their wish. What Stalin did in the late 1930s was thus simply a return to the pre-revolutionary tsarist foreign and national policy (for example, the Russian colonization of Siberia and Muslim Asia was no longer condemned as imperialist expansion, but was celebrated as the introduction of progressive modernization). In a similar way, Putin brought together his security council in February 2022 and asked each of its members whether they supported the decision to recognize the independence of the self-proclaimed republics of Donetsk and Luhansk. According to *El País*, when his turn came, Sergei Naryshkin, the foreign intelligence chief,

> first suggests that the West be given one last chance to return to the Minsk agreements, which could be done by giving the

West a short-term ultimatum. Putin interrupts him dryly: 'What does that mean? Are you suggesting we start negotiations or recognize sovereignty?' Naryshkin starts to stutter, he doesn't know what to say, he mumbles 'yes' then 'no,' and his face turns white for seconds that seem to last an eternity. 'Speak clearly,' Putin interjects. Feeling the pressure, the spy chief does a U-turn and goes one step further: he says he supports the annexation of Donetsk and Luhansk into the Russian Federation. But he is again called out by Putin: 'We're not talking about that. We're talking about recognizing their independence or not. Yes or no?' So the nervous Naryshkin takes back what he said once again: yes, yes, he supports it. 'Thanks, you can take your seat.'[17]

Naryshkin confused the script: first, he proposed a too-mild version (just offer another ultimatum to the West), and then, in an act of obvious panic, he went too far and said that he supported their integration into Russia ... As the *El Pais* commentator put it: 'The dramatic intensity of the scene would make it stand out in any movie or piece of fiction, but it's not fiction.' This scene tells us more about the situation in Russian top circles than a heap of secret reports that have since been released – Naryshkin, the head of foreign intelligence, the guy whom everybody should fear because of the data he may possess, stutters with his face blank and is then told to take his seat as a disgraced schoolboy who has finally muttered the right answer. This is how 'hearing the voice of the people' works in Russia today.[18] Rarely in today's era of perfected manipulation are we given the chance to see so openly how this mechanism works – in the West, we learned to use it more subtly.

It is crucial to bear in mind that the ongoing invasion of Ukraine is the final act of a long struggle to eliminate the

Leninist tradition in Russia. The last time Lenin made headlines in the West was during the Ukrainian uprising in 2014, which toppled the pro-Russian president Yanukovich: in TV reports on the mass protests in Kiev, we saw again and again the scenes of enraged protesters tearing down statues of Lenin. These furious attacks were understandable insofar as Lenin's statues functioned as a symbol of the Soviet oppression, and Putin's Russia was perceived as a continuation of the Soviet policy of subjecting non-Russian nations to Russian domination. There was nonetheless a deep irony to Ukrainians tearing down Lenin's statues as a sign of their desire to assert national sovereignty: the golden era of Ukraine's national identity was not the pre-Leninist era of Tsarist Russia (when Ukrainian national self-assertion was thwarted), but the first decade of the Soviet Union, when they established a fully fledged national identity. Throughout the 1920s, the Soviet policy of 'korenization' (literally, *indigenization*) encouraged a revival of Ukrainian culture and language; this, combined with progressive measures – universal healthcare, improved labour, housing and women's rights, and so on – contributed to a flourishing Ukrainian state. These policy gains were reversed once Stalin consolidated power in the early 1930s, hitting Ukraine in a particularly brutal way – suffice it to recall the infamous Holodomor, the terror-famine from 1932 to 1933 that killed millions of Ukrainians, and also the fact that, in just two years of *yezhovshchina* (the Great Terror of 1936–7), only three out of 200 members of the Central Committee of the Ukraine Republic survived.[19] Ukraine's 'indigenization', cruelly undone by Stalin, had followed principles formulated by Lenin in quite unambiguous terms:

The proletariat cannot but fight against the forcible retention of the oppressed nations within the boundaries of a given state, and this is exactly what the struggle for the right of self-determination means. The proletariat must demand the right of political secession for the colonies and for the nations that 'its own' nation oppresses. Unless it does this, proletarian internationalism will remain a meaningless phrase; mutual confidence and class solidarity between the workers of the oppressing and oppressed nations will be impossible.[20]

Lenin remained faithful to this position to the end: in his last struggle against Stalin's project for the centralized Soviet Union, he again advocated the unconditional right of small nations to secede (in this case, Georgia was at stake), insisting on the full sovereignty of the national entities that composed the Soviet State – no wonder that, on September 27 1922, in a letter to the members of the Politburo, Stalin openly accused Lenin of 'national liberalism'. Today, Putin's foreign policy is a clear continuation of this tsarist-Stalinist line: after the Russian Revolution of 1917, according to Putin, it was the turn of the Bolsheviks to aggrieve Russia:

> Ruling with your ideas as a guide is correct, but that is only the case when that idea leads to the right results, not like it did with Vladimir Ilyich. In the end that idea led to the ruin of the Soviet Union. There were many of these ideas such as providing regions with autonomy, and so on. They planted an atomic bomb under the building that is called Russia which would later explode.[21]

In short, Lenin is guilty of taking seriously the autonomy of different nations that composed the Russian empire, of questioning Russian hegemony. Trotsky faithfully followed Lenin's path – the two subtitles of his April 1939 article 'Problem of the

Ukraine'[22] tell it all: 'For a Free, Independent Soviet Ukraine!', and 'Soviet Constitution Admits Right of Self-Determination'. He takes this to its logical conclusion: 'But the independence of a United Ukraine would mean the separation of Soviet Ukraine from the USSR, the "friends" of the Kremlin will exclaim in chorus. What is so terrible about that? we reply.' This is true proletarian internationalism!

In his last speech, in 1952, Stalin praised Palmiro Togliatti and Maurice Thorez – leaders of the Italian and French communist parties – for their 'internationalism', because they had declared that, if the Soviet Army entered their countries, they would not fight it. This is the 'internationalism' today's Russia expects from Ukraine! No wonder that we once again see Stalin's portraits during Russian military parades and public celebrations, while Lenin is obliterated; in a large opinion poll from a couple of years ago, Stalin was voted the third greatest Russian of all time, while Lenin was nowhere to be seen. Stalin is not celebrated as a Communist, but as the restorer of Russia's greatness after Lenin's anti-patriotic 'deviation'. No wonder that, on 21 February 2022, announcing his military 'intervention' in the Donbas region, Putin repeated his old claim that Lenin, who rose to power after the downfall of the Romanov royal family, was the 'author and creator' of Ukraine.[23] Can we put things more clearly? All those Leftists who still have a soft heart for Russia (after all, Russia is the successor of the Soviet Union, Western democracies are a fake, and Putin opposes US imperialism . . .) should fully accept the brutal fact that Putin is a conservative nationalist. The US and Russia are superpowers in decline, and their conservative nationalism is all the more dangerous because it is so frail. What we need more than ever is true proletarian internationalism, and we have seen traces of it in Ukraine in the months since Russia invaded.

The Perverted Normality of War (and Peace)

In Russian, when rhythm is given by the commanding officer for soldiers to march along to, he shouts, 'Raz, dva, raz, dva . . .' ('one, two, one, two . . .', or 'left, right, left, right . . .'). I was told in Moscow years ago that Putin is often referred to as 'Dvaputin' – 'Rasputin, Dvaputin'. And Dvaputin is, for sure, worse than Rasputin who, at the beginning of the Great War, warned the Tsarist family that, due to the poverty and suffering of the large majority of its population, Russia's full engagement in the war might lead to the fall of the entire political system. Today, Russia is facing the same situation – and Dvaputin would do well to listen to the advice of whoever today's Rasputin is.

With the Russian invasion of Ukraine, we have entered a new phase of what war means. What is new is not just that both sides have nuclear arms and that a new rhetoric is emerging (Putin has made it clear that Russia is ready to use nuclear weapons first). We are approaching a perfect storm, in which a whole series of catastrophes (pandemics, global warming, food and water shortages, war . . .) are strengthening each other, meaning that the question is not simply one of war or peace but rather of whether we will adapt to a global state of emergency in which our priorities must change all the time. What needs an explanation is the basic madness of the situation: at a time when it is generally agreed that our very survival is under threat for ecological reasons, and when everything we are doing should be subordinated to cope with this danger, all of a sudden the prime concern has become a new war that can only shorten our passage to collective suicide. At a time when global cooperation is needed more than ever, the 'clash of civilizations'has returned with a vengeance. To explain this through the interests of big capital and state control falls short. As is often the case, we need to go back to Hegel's philosophy.

Does one of the most famous passages in Hegel's *Phenomenology*, the dialectic of master and servant, not signal where we are today? If, in the confrontation of two self-consciousnesses engaged in a life-and-death struggle, both parties are ready to risk their lives, if they both persist to the bitter end, there can be no winner. One will die, and one will survive but without the other to recognize them. The whole history of freedom, struggle and recognition – in short, the whole of history, the whole of human culture – can take place only with an original compromise: in the final face-off, one side (the future servant) must 'avert its eyes', not ready to go to the end.

The threat of violence always looms over every master–servant relationship, but it remains an exception, a threat that occasionally explodes in rebellions, while, as Hegel knew very well, there is no such compromise-resolution in the relations between nation-states: the co-existence of sovereign states implies the necessity of war. Each state disciplines its own members and guarantees civic peace among them, but the relationship between different states is permanently under the shadow of potential war, with each epoch of peace nothing more than a temporary armistice. As Hegel conceptualized it, the entire ethic of a state culminates in the highest act of heroism, the readiness to sacrifice one's life for one's nation-state, which means that the wild barbarian relations between states serve as the foundation of the ethical life within each one. Is today's North Korea, with its ruthless pursuit of nuclear weapons and rockets, not the ultimate expression of this logic of unconditional nation-state sovereignty?

There are clear signs that China is also moving in this direction. I have been informed by friends in China (who shall remain unnamed) that, in Chinese popular military journals, many writers have complained that the Chinese army needs a real war to test its fighting ability – while the US army is permanently doing so in Iraq, Somalia, the Maghreb, and so on. China hasn't, they lament, had the chance to do this for decades, not since its short, failed intervention in Vietnam. The bigger official media outlets have, of late, openly claimed that, since the prospect of peaceful integration of Taiwan into China is dwindling, what is needed is a military liberation of the island. As a form of ideological preparation for this moment, patriotism and suspicion about everything foreign is growing, accompanied by accusations that the US wants a war in Taiwan. In the autumn of 2021, the top authorities advised the population to stock their homes with enough food to survive for two months in case, due to a non-specified trouble, food distribution was disturbed[24] – a strange warning, which was generally perceived as announcing an imminent war. I should also mention here the Chinese mega-hit film *The Battle at Lake Changjin*, which was released in 2021 to mark 100 years of the Chinese Communist Party. It celebrates China's intervention in the Korean war in 1950. The following March, Foreign Minister Wang Yi asserted that China's (falsely neutral, *de facto* pro-Russian) stance on Ukraine was 'objective, fair and consistent with the wishes of most countries', and that 'time will prove China's stance is on the right side of history.'[25] My reaction: it's quite possible that 'time will prove' this – in the sense that the anti-Ukrainian interpretation will prevail in many parts of the world. But I wouldn't like to live in a world where such a lie prevails over the truth.

This tendency to establish national sovereignty through violence and war runs directly against the pressing need for us to establish a new mode of relating to our environment, a radical politico-economic change called by Peter Sloterdijk 'the domestication of the wild animal culture'. The moment we fully accept the fact that we live on a Spaceship Earth, the task that urgently imposes itself is that of civilizing civilizations themselves, of imposing universal solidarity and cooperation among all human communities, a task rendered all the more difficult by the ongoing rise of sectarian religious and ethnic 'heroic' violence and readiness to sacrifice oneself (and the world) for one's specific cause. More than a year ago, Alain Badiou wrote that the contours of the future war are already drawn:

> the United States and their Western-Japanese group on the one side, China and Russia on the other side, atomic arms everywhere. We cannot but recall Lenin's statement: 'Either revolution will prevent the war or war will trigger revolution.' This is how we can define the maximal ambition of the political work to come: for the first time in history, the first hypothesis – revolution will prevent the war – should realize itself, and not the second one – a war will trigger revolution. It is effectively the second hypothesis which materialized itself in Russia in the context of the First World War, and in China in the context of the second. But at what price! And with what long-term consequences![26]

There is no way to avoid the conclusion that a radical social change – a revolution – is needed to civilize our civilizations.

We cannot afford to hope that a new war will lead to this revolution: a new war would much more probably mean the end of civilization as we know it, with the survivors (if any) organized in small authoritarian groups. And we should have no illusions here: in some basic sense the Third World War has already begun, although it has until now mostly been fought through proxies. The sooner we admit this, the better chances we have of preventing its full explosion. (We should also bear in mind that China is already part of the ongoing war, helping Russia financially and economically.)

We all want peace, but abstract calls for peace are not enough: 'peace' alone is not a term that allows us to draw the key political distinction. Occupiers always sincerely want peace in the territory they hold. Germany definitely wanted peace in occupied France in the early 1940s, Israel wants peace on the occupied West Bank, and Russia is on a mission for peace in Ukraine. That's why, as Étienne Balibar put it in an honestly brutal way, today 'pacifism is not an option.'[27] We should prevent a new great war, but the only way to do it is to engage in a total mobilization against today's vision of 'peace', which can only be maintained through local wars. Recall that, after the fall of the Soviet Union, Cuba proclaimed a 'special period in times of peace' (*'periodo especial en tiempos de paz'*), meaning: wartime conditions in a time of peace. Maybe this is the term we should use for our predicament today.

On whom or what can we rely to guide us through such conditions? Artists and thinkers? Pragmatic *Realpolitik*? Artists and thinkers can also lay the foundation for wars and crimes. At their most innocent, we get from artists ambiguous platitudes. On 24 February 2022, the actor AnnaLynne McCord published a video in which she read a slam poem addressed to Putin, which begins, 'Dear President Vladimir Putin, I'm so sorry I was not your mother,' and goes on to explain how, if she was his mother, she would have showered him with love so that he would not be inclined to start wars.[28] This poem is just plainly wrong: the problem with big criminals is precisely that they were showered with too much maternal love, which deprived them of free breathing space.

But things can get much worse than that. Recall William Butler Yeats' well-known lines:

> I have spread my dreams under your feet;
> Tread softly because you tread on my dreams.

We should apply these lines to poets themselves: when they are spreading their dreams under our feet, they should spread them carefully because actual people will read them and act upon them – the same Yeats was continuously flirting with Fascism, in August 1938 publicly approving of the anti-Semitic Nuremberg Laws. There is no ethnic cleansing without poetry – why? Because we live in an era that perceives itself as post-ideological. Since great ideological causes (freedom, social justice, free education) no longer have the force to mobilize people for mass violence, a larger sacred cause is needed, which makes petty individual concerns about killing seem trivial. Religion or ethnic belonging fit this role perfectly. Of course, there are cases of pathological atheists who are able to commit mass murder just for pleasure, but they are rare exceptions: the majority needs to be anaesthetized against their elementary sensitivity to others' suffering, and for this, a sacred Cause is needed. Religious ideologues usually claim that, true or not, religion makes otherwise bad people do good things; judging from today's experience, we should rather stick to Steve Weinberg's claim that, while, without religion, good people would have been doing good things and bad people bad things, only religion can make good people do bad things. Plato's reputation suffers because of his claim that poets should be thrown out of the city – but this is rather sensible advice, given that, in recent decades, so much ethnic cleansing has been ushered in by the dangerous dreams of poets and 'thinkers' (in Russia, for example, by Aleksandr Dugin's books and Nikita Mikhalkov's films). There is only a short step from *Dichter und Denker* (poet and thinker) to *Richter und Henker* (judge and hangman) – so, perhaps, we should supplement Anna Kamienska's well-known line that 'poetry is a presentiment of the truth' with: 'Yes, but this truth can also be the truth about the darkest drives that dwell hidden in our mind.' To paraphrase Thackeray, poetry can make darlings of our ugliest thoughts.

With *Realpolitik*, things are almost worse. Political pragmatism or 'realism' is powerless to respond to the mystifications of ideology: precisely when it denounces the simplifications or naivety of an ideology, it ignores the mystifications involved in its own 'realist' position – how, exactly? Ideology often evokes some hidden dimension behind the veil of appearances in order to cover up the crime that is being openly committed (and legitimized by ideology). The favoured expression that announces such double mystification is 'the situation is more complex'. An obvious fact – let's say, a brutal military aggression – is relativized by evoking a 'much more complex situation in the background', which, usually, makes the aggression an act of defence. Is this not exactly what is happening in Ukraine? Russia brutally attacks Ukraine, but many commentators are searching for the 'complexity' behind the attack. Yes, for sure there is complexity there, but the basic fact remains: Russia did it. Our mistake was not taking Putin's threats literally enough – we thought he didn't really mean what he said, and was just playing a game of strategic manipulation. The supreme irony is that one cannot but recall here the famous Jewish joke, quoted by Freud, in which a lie assumes the form of factual truth. 'Why are you telling me you are going to Lviv when you are really going to Lviv?' one friend asks another. The pair have established an implicit code that, when you go to Lviv, you say that you are going to Cracow, and vice versa; within this framework, telling the literal truth means lying. When Putin announced military intervention, we didn't take Putin's declaration that he wanted to 'pacify' and 'denazify' all of Ukraine literally enough, so the reproach of the disappointed strategists is now, 'Why were you telling us you were going to occupy Lviv when you really wanted to occupy Lviv?' In other words, what this double mystification implies is the end of *Realpolitik* as we knew it: 'enacting or engaging in diplomatic or political policies based primarily on considerations of given circumstances and factors, rather than strictly binding itself to explicit ideological notions or moral and ethical premises'.[29] Such *Realpolitik* is as a rule opposed to naivety, i.e. to naively binding ourselves on (our version of) moral or political principles. However, in a situation like today's, to play such *Realpolitik* is precisely too naive: its basic presupposition (that the other side, the enemy, is also aiming at a pragmatic deal) can no longer be relied on.

During the Cold War, the rules of international behaviour were clear, guaranteed by the MADness (Mutually Assured Destruction) of the superpowers: each side could be sure that, if it decided to launch a nuclear attack, the other side would respond with full destructive force, ensuring neither side would start a war. However, since Kim Jong-Un has begun to talk about dealing a devastating blow to the US, we cannot but wonder where he sees his own position. He speaks as if he were not aware that his country, himself included, would be destroyed in this scenario, that is, he talks as if he were playing a fantasy game whose name is NUTS (Nuclear Utilization Target Selection) – as though, by means of a surgical strike, you could destroy the enemy's nuclear capacities while an anti-missile shield protected you from a counter-strike. In recent decades, even the US has oscillated between MAD and NUTS: it acts as if it continues to trust the MAD logic in its relations with Russia and China, while it is tempted to consider a NUTS approach with Iran and North Korea. With his hints at the possible use of nuclear weapons, Putin follows the same reasoning. The very fact that two directly contradictory strategies are mobilized simultaneously by the same superpower bears witness to the fantasy character of this entire reasoning.

Today, then, we are beyond MADness: superpowers are testing each other, trying to impose their own version of global rules, experimenting with them through proxies, which, of course, are other small nations and states. In the weeks after the invasion began, Putin said that the Western sanctions introduced on his country were the 'equivalent of a declaration of war'. We should read this statement together with what Putin repeatedly said during the first months of the war: economic exchange with the West should go on as normal, Russia is keeping its commitments and continuing its gas deliveries to Western Europe. Now that Europe has successfully reduced its dependence on Russian gas, it has become clear that Russia was trying to impose a new model of international relations: not cold war but hot peace, a peace that equals a permanent hybrid war, where military interventions are declared to be 'peacekeeping' humanitarian missions against genocide. When the war started, we read that 'the state Duma expresses its unequivocal and consolidated support for the adequate measures taken for humanitarian purposes.' How often in the past have we heard similar phrases applied to Western interventions, from Latin America to Iraq? Now, Russia is belatedly taking this language over. While city shelling, civilian killings, and the destruction of everything from universities to maternity wards is unfolding in Ukraine, international commerce should continue; outside Ukraine, normal life should go on – and does go on. So we have a permanent global peace that is permanently sustained by 'peacekeeping military interventions'. No wonder that, since the Russian media are banned from using the term 'war' to describe what the Russian army is doing in Ukraine, and have been ordered to refer to it as a 'special military operation', a joke is already circulating that there will be a new edition of Tolstoy's classic novel with the title *A Special Military Operation and Peace*.

Can we be free in such a predicament? In English there are two words, 'freedom' and 'liberty', that refer to the same thing. Let me take a risk and fix this opposition as the one between what Hegel called 'abstract freedom' and 'concrete freedom'. Abstract freedom is the ability to do what one wants independently of social rules and customs, to violate these rules and customs, exemplarily in a revolt or revolutionary situation. Concrete freedom is the freedom sustained by a set of rules and customs. In our daily lives we mostly rely on the latter. I can walk freely along a busy street because I can be reasonably sure that others on the street will behave in a civilized way towards me, and will be punished if they attack or insult me. I can only exert the freedom to speak and communicate with others if I obey the commonly established rules of language (with all their ambiguities, including the unwritten rules of reading messages 'between the lines'). The language we speak is, of course, not ideologically neutral: it embodies many prejudices and makes it impossible for us to formulate clearly certain uncommon thoughts. Thinking always occurs in language and brings with it a common-sense metaphysics (view of reality). To truly think, we have to think in a language against this language, i.e., we have to mobilize our abstract freedom.

There are moments of crisis when abstract freedom has to intervene in a much more brutal way. In December 1944, Jean-Paul Sartre wrote:

> Never were we freer than under the German occupation. We had lost all our rights, and first of all our right to speak. They insulted us to our faces. . . . And that is why the Resistance was a true democracy; for the soldier, as for his superior, the same danger, the same loneliness, the same responsibility, the same absolute freedom within the discipline.[30]

This situation, full of anxiety and danger, was abstract freedom, not concrete liberty – liberty was established when post-war normality returned. So, in Ukraine today, those who fight the Russian invasion have abstract freedom and fight for concrete liberty – but can we still maintain this distinction clearly? Are we not increasingly approaching a situation in which millions of people think that they have to act freely (to violate the rules) in order to protect their liberty? Is this not why a Trumpian mob invaded the Capitol on 6 January 2021?

How did we get into this mess? We live in a strange world for which we still lack a proper word. The philosopher Catherine Malabou[31] sees cryptocurrencies as a sign that the global capitalist system 'is beginning its anarchist turn . . . How else are we to describe such phenomena as decentralized currencies, the end of the state's monopoly, the obsolescence of the mediating role played by banks, and the decentralization of exchanges and transactions?' Sounds nice; but, as Malabou immediately points out, 'the semantics of anarchism that give ultra-capitalism its new tonality changes nothing as regards the logic of profit, which ultra-capitalism only expresses in a different form.' With the gradual disappearance of the state's monopoly, the limits to ruthless exploitation and domination imposed by the state also disappear. The original idea of cryptocurrencies as a new space of freedom without external control of some authority ends up in what Malabou herself calls 'the combination – at once sense-less, monstrous, and unprecedented – of *savage verticality* and *uncontrollable horizontality.*' Today's anarcho-capitalism aims at transparency, but the paradox of a discourse of transparency is that it 'simultaneously authorizes the large-scale but opaque use of data, the dark web, and the fabrication of information'. To prevent this descent into chaos, savage verticality also takes the form of the Fascist evolution of so many of today's govern-ments' policies, with the excessive security and military build-up that goes along with it. Such phenomena do not contradict a drive towards anarchism. Rather, they indicate precisely the dis-appearance of the state, which, once its social function has been removed, expresses the obsolescence of its force through the use of violence. Ultra-nationalism thus signals the death agony of national authority.

With regard to Ukraine, this means that what we are dealing with is not one nation-state attacking another nation-state: Ukraine is attacked as an entity whose very existence is denied by the aggressor, and whose government is disqualified as a group of drug-addicted neo-Nazis. Russia justifies its attack using the terms of geopolitical 'spheres of influence', which often reach well beyond national borders (is China not show-ing signs of doing the same, announcing a peacekeeping mission in Taiwan and securing its sphere of influence in the

South Chinese Sea?). This is why Russia doesn't use the term 'war' for its military intervention in Ukraine: not just to down-play the brutality of its intervention but above all to make it clear that war in the old sense of an armed conflict between nation-states no longer applies. Russia is just securing 'peace' in what it considers its own geopolitical sphere of influence, and such 'peacekeeping' can easily spread well beyond Ukraine.

In March 2022, the Russian ambassador to Bosnia, Igor Kalabukhov, took this 'peacekeeping' a step further: he said that Bosnia had the right to decide whether or not to join NATO, but that Moscow also reserved the right to 'respond to such a possibility in accordance with its interest'. He con-tinued, 'If [Bosnia] decides to be a member of any alliance, that is an internal matter. Our response is a different matter. Ukraine's example shows what we expect. Should there be any threat, we will respond.'[32] His mention of Ukraine gave a clear hint of what this 'response' would be. The Russian Foreign Minister Sergey Lavrov demanded that NATO should with-draw from all countries that joined in or after 1997,[33] with further hints that the full solution would be to demilitarize all of Europe.[34] So Russia with its army will be maintaining peace there with occasional humanitarian interventions – and Dmitry Medvedev made the same point in March 2023, claiming that 'the only way to secure lasting peace with Ukraine is to push the border of hostile countries as far as Poland, if necessary.'[35] Similar ideas abound in the Russian press – Dmitry Evstafiev, a political commentator and opinion maker, said in an interview with Czech media:

A new Russia is born which lets you know clearly that it doesn't perceive you, Europe, as a partner. Russia has three partners: USA, China, and India. You are for us a trophy which shall be divided between us and Americans. You didn't yet get this, although we are coming close to this.[36]

Evstafiev pointedly excludes Europe from the list of four big players, perfectly in line with the old mantra of opposing 'Eurocentrism' – a habit that bothers many across the entire political spectrum, from the anti-colonialist Left to the populist Right. This objection to the idea of a *united* Europe is curious; for all the justified critique of key parts of the European legacy, what appears to make Europe an object of hatred and envy is the fact that, in the eyes of many, 'Europe' still stands for truly peaceful cooperation of nations, personal freedom, and the welfare state.

So when the Ukrainian government repeatedly declares that the country want to be part of Europe, we should ask ourselves what they see in 'Europe', and whether we are ready to live up to their expectations. Whichever way you look at it, a united Europe stands for some kind of social democracy, which is why Viktor Orbán in a recent interview went so far as to proclaim that the Western liberal hegemony 'is gradually becoming Marxist':

Sooner or later we'll have to face up to the fact that, opposing the Christian democratic camp, we're no longer dealing with a group espousing liberal ideology, but with a group that's essentially Marxist with liberal remnants. This is what we have in America today. For the time being the conservative side is at a disadvantage in relation to the Marxist, liberal camp.[37]

This is the predominant meaning of 'anti-Eurocentrism' today.

On the afternoon of 1 March 2022, on a video-call to the European parliament, Zelensky said: 'Ukraine is ready to die for Europe. Now let's see if Europe is ready to die for Ukraine.' The moment he said this, the hearts of almost all of the European extreme Right (which up to that point had displayed sympathy for Russia's intervention) began to beat for Ukraine: Salvini, Marine le Pen and others made a quick U-turn and began to advocate full support for receiving refugees and sending arms to Ukraine. Why? As one commentator put it, 'Dying for the homeland has always been the dream of the nationalists, although this does not mean that they really want to die personally. They want to send someone to die for their glory: yes, that's their dream.'[38] If it's only the threat of war that can mobilize us, not the threat to our environment, then the liberty we will get if our side wins is perhaps not worth living. So it seems we are facing an impossible choice where both options are worse: if we make compromises in the name of maintaining peace we will be feeding a Russian appetite for expansionism that only the 'demilitarization' of all of Europe will satisfy; if we endorse an all-out military confrontation, we run the high risk of a new world war. The only real solution to this debilitating dilemma is to change the entire terrain – to transform the way we perceive the situation.

The problem is, while the global liberal-capitalist order is obviously approaching a crisis at many levels, the war in Ukraine is now again falsely simplified into barbaric-totalitarian countries versus the civilized free West – putting global warming and other global problems safely out of sight. We could even go so far as to say that the new wars do not simply ignore climate change and other global trouble; they are, rather, a reaction to our global problems, a return to a perverted 'normality' of war. The idea being: OK, there are difficult times ahead, so let's grab a strong position in order to survive the forthcoming challenges better than others. The present time is thus not a moment of truth when things become clear, when the basic antagonism is clearly seen. It is a moment of the deepest lie. So while we should firmly stand behind Ukraine, we should avoid the fascination with the prospect of war that is clearly present among those who keep pushing towards an open confrontation with Russia – whose argument could be summed up like this: 'Finally, all the pseudo-struggles for women's rights and against racism that were tearing us apart are out of sight, and all the babble about the crisis of capitalism is deservedly marginalized, and the men are now once again required to act like men and fight. This is why women and children are leaving Ukraine, while men are returning there to do their job!' This is not even to mention the spontaneous expressions of racism throughout European and American reporting on Ukraine, which has been widely noted. In the first week of the invasion, CBS News correspondent Charlie D'Agata said that Ukraine 'isn't a place, with all due respect, like Iraq or Afghanistan, that has seen conflict raging for decades. This is a relatively civilized, relatively European – I have to choose those words carefully, too – city, one where you wouldn't expect that, or hope that it's going to happen'. A former deputy prosecutor general of Ukraine told the BBC: 'It's very emotional for me because I see European people with blue eyes and blond hair . . . being killed every day.' A French journalist, Phillipe Corbé, stated: 'We're not talking here about Syrians fleeing the bombing of the Syrian regime backed by Putin. We're talking about Europeans leaving in cars that look like ours to save their lives.'[39] Beyond the blatant racism of these comments, is it not curious that we are forgetting our complicity in these conflicts? Today, when Afghanistan is really an Islamic fundamentalist country, few seem to still remember that, forty years ago, it was a country with strong secular traditions . . . But then first the Soviet Union and then the US intervened, and now we are where we are.

Such racism strangely echoes the stance of Patriarch Kirill of Moscow, head of the Russian Orthodox Church, who often addresses military leaders and even published a statement in honour of Defender of the Fatherland Day. The cleric congratulated Putin on his 'high and responsible service to the people of Russia', declaring that the Russian Orthodox Church has 'always striven to make a significant contribution to the patriotic education of compatriots', and lauding military service as 'an active manifestation of evangelical love for neighbours'.[40] If we just seek to 'defend Europe', we are already speaking Putin's language. The line between civilization and barbarism is internal to civilizations, which is why our struggle is universal. The only true universality today is the universality of struggle. So while Ukraine's struggle deserves full support, something like a new non-aligned movement is needed – not in the sense that we should be neutral in the ongoing war but in the sense that we should question the entire notion of the 'clash of civilizations'.

According to Samuel Huntington, after the end of the Cold War the 'iron curtain of ideology' has been replaced by the 'velvet curtain of culture' as the most significant dividing line in Europe. Huntington's dark vision of a looming 'clash of civilizations' may appear to be the very opposite of Francis Fukuyama's bright prospect of the End of History in the guise of a worldwide liberal democracy – for what could be more different from Fukuyama's pseudo-Hegelian idea that the final formula of the best possible social order was found in capitalist liberal democracy, than a political struggle between rival nations? How do these two ideas fit together? From today's experience, the answer is clear: *the clash of civilizations IS politics at the end of history.* Today's identity-led, ethno-religious conflicts are the form of struggle that best fits global capitalism today: in our age of 'post-politics' when politics proper is progressively replaced by expert social administration, the only remaining legitimate sources of conflict are cultural (ethnic, religious) tensions. The rise of 'irrational' violence strictly correlates with the depoliticization of our societies. Within this horizon, the only alternative to war remains the peaceful coexistence of civilizations (of different 'truths', as Dugin put it, or of 'ways of life', a more popular term today), wherein forced marriages and homophobia (or the idea that a woman alone in public is asking for rape) are OK, provided that they occur within the borders of another country which is otherwise fully integrated into the world market.

This is not what non-alignment means today. Non-alignment means that our struggle should be universal. That's why we should avoid Russophobia at all costs, and give all our support to those who are protesting in Russia against the invasion of Ukraine: in displaying their internationalism they are the true Russian patriots. A patriot, a person who really loves her or his country, is someone who is deeply ashamed of it when it does something bad. There is no more disgusting saying than: 'My country, right or wrong.'

The Fifth Rider of the Apocalypse

One of the implications of true global solidarity is that it should not be limited to its secular-liberal, Western form. What does this mean in practice? In late March 2022, Aleksandr Dugin gave a long interview to the tabloid *Moskovskij Komsomolets*, Russia's highest-circulation daily; when asked if Putin reads his work, he said, 'I think we read the same letters written in gold in the sky of Russian history,' and then he went on to quote some of these golden letters:

> We are waging an eschatological military operation, a special operation between Light and Darkness in the situation of the end of times. Truth and God are on our side. We are fighting the absolute evil embodied in Western civilization, its liberal-totalitarian hegemony, in Ukrainian Nazism.[41]

My counterpoint is not just that I, for obvious reasons, don't trust people who read 'letters written in gold in the sky'. There are other details that deserve our attention in the quoted lines, especially the jump from Western liberalism to Nazism – the phrase 'liberal-totalitarian hegemony' is on a par with the Nazi term 'Jewish-Bolshevik conspiracy'. And why is the enemy 'Ukrainian Nazism'? Well, because Putin replaced the October Revolution with the Soviet Union's victory in the Second World War (and the enormous cost of winning the war – 25 million dead) as the new founding myth of Russia's greatness. That's another reason why Stalin's image can be seen on display throughout military parades– he is celebrated as the supreme commander, not as a Communist. But since today's enemy is Western liberalism, Nazism has to appear as liberalism's ultimate offspring.

Beyond this, two other important features are clearly discernible in the quoted passage. First, the military-religious link: Russia's 'military operation' is explicitly characterized in terms proper to theology, as a fight between Truth/God and absolute Evil that is not a simple historical event but which takes place in the end times. Even the most radical Muslim fundamentalists do not talk like that. Second, Dugin here violates his own postmodern relativism according to which, 'every so-called truth is a matter of believing. So we believe in what we do, we believe in what we say. And that is the only way to define the truth. So we have our special Russian truth that you need to accept.'[42] In the quoted interview, he doesn't talk about 'Russian Truth' versus 'European Truth' as he has elsewhere, but about Light and Darkness, God versus absolute Evil.

However, is it enough to oppose such militarized religion by cleaving to peaceful, everyday secular liberalism, which sets out to tolerate different ways of life? Today, when we are de facto already living in an emergency state, mobilization *is* needed; and why should we forfeit religious references to neo-Fascists? Somewhere towards the end of April 2022, the global public became aware of a deep change in how the Ukrainian war was playing out. The dream of a quick resolution was over: the war became strangely 'normalized', accepted as a process that would go on and become part of our lives for some time to come. The fear of a much stronger conflict began to penetrate our daily life – a friend from Sweden told me that the authorities were instructing all households to store provisions (food, medicines, and so on) that would enable them to survive wartime conditions.

The Russian view – that this is a global conflict – has been articulated more and more explicitly: Europe is turning Nazi, and as such the war in Ukraine is *de facto* the beginning of a Third World War. As Margarita Simonyan, the head of *Russia Today*, put it: 'Either we lose in Ukraine, or a third world war begins. Personally, I think the scenario of a third world war is more realistic.'[43] No wonder that Russian TV channels are now flooded with calls to commit greater resources to Ukraine and 'fight NATO'. Special Forces veteran Alexander Arutyu-nov asked Putin directly: 'Dear Vladimir Vladimirovich, please decide, are we fighting a war or are we masturbating? We need to stop this dry handjob.'[44] (Note, again, the sexual metaphor, which is constantly present in Russian propaganda: enough jerking off, let's really rape Ukraine . . .) And so we hurtle towards a crazy vision of a united liberal-totalitarian Nazi-Jewish plot. A few months into the war, in an interview on the Italian TV programme *Zona Bianca*, Sergei Lavrov was asked how Russia could claim that it is fighting to 'de-Nazify' Ukraine when Zelensky is himself Jewish. Lavrov replied: 'I could be wrong, but Hitler also had Jewish blood. [That Zelensky is Jewish] means absolutely nothing. Wise Jewish people say that the most ardent anti-Semites are usually Jews.'[45] (Incidentally, who are these 'wise Jewish people'? The only ones I know are fervent Zionists who accuse Jews critical of Israeli politics on the West Bank of being 'self-hating' . . .)

Russia isn't just trying to dismantle a united Europe, though – it is now engaged in a strategy to present itself as an ally of the Third World against Western neocolonialism, casting the attack on Ukraine as an act of decolonization.[46] Russian propa-ganda ably manipulates bitter memories of how Western powers acted throughout Africa, Asia and the Middle East: was the bombing of Iraq not worse than the bombing of Kyiv? Russia combines this vision of itself as the agent of global decolonization with discreet (or even not so discreet) military support for local dictators in Syria, the Central African Republic, and elsewhere. Plus, beneath Russia's demand that its oil and gas should be paid for in Rubles is a gigantic attempt, coordinated with China, to depose the US dollar and euro as global currencies. We should not underestimate the efficiency of these strategies: when Ukraine proudly declares that it defends Europe, Russia's reply is: yes, and we defend all of Europe's past and present victims. In Serbia we have begun to see the results of this propaganda campaign: according to the latest opinion polls, more than 60 per cent of voters now oppose the country's entry into the European Union.

If Europe wants to stand a chance of winning this ideological war, it should do nothing less than radically transform its model of liberal-capitalist globalization – nothing else will do the job. If Europe fails to do this, it may survive as an island (really, a 'fortress') surrounded by enemies who will slowly penetrate it. In 'Liberalism Needs the Nation',[47] an op-ed written in the wake of the Russian invasion of Ukraine, Francis Fukuyama pointed out how the patriotic defence of one's country can also function as a defence of liberal notions – it all depends on which values one's 'nation' represents. Does the last century not already offer numerous examples of a radical-Left patriotic struggle against foreign domination?

On the opposite side, in Western Europe, especially in Germany, we have a new version of pacifism. If we cut the noble rhetorical crap, the message of these new pacifists is roughly this: bearing in mind our economic interests, as well as the danger of showing too much support for Ukraine and thus getting enmeshed in a military conflict, we should allow Ukraine to be swallowed by Russia, and limit ourselves to peaceful protests and shows of sympathy. What is this 'too much'? It is the fear of crossing the threshold beyond which Russia will get really angry at our sympathy for Ukraine – but this is being continually defined *and redefined* by Putin, and playing on this fear is part of Putin's strategy. I agree that we should prevent the full outbreak of a new World War, but sometimes being too cautious only provokes the aggressor, who counts on our reluctance to resist. So we should also be ready to draw a line ourselves precisely to prevent an all-out war. Remember how, after Putin announced the intervention in Ukraine, Biden's first reaction was that we would have to see whether this was a case of a limited occupation of the Donbas region, or a full occupation of Ukraine? This was not a very wise move, because he thereby gave the signal that a limited intervention would be tolerable.

But behind this reversal there is a much sadder insight. Voices of the pacifist European Left warn against the return of the heroic-military spirit, and Jurgen Habermas has even talked about Ukraine morally blackmailing Europe.[48] There is something deeply melancholic in Habermas's otherwise well-thought out reaction: he is fully aware that, after the Second World War, Europe was able to renounce militarism only because it was kept safe under the US nuclear umbrella, and he knows that, with the Russian attack on Ukraine, this time is over – that unconditional pacifism can now only be sustained through more and more compromise. Europe's former liberal pacifism, its apathy, is running out of its time, and, unfortunately, 'heroic' acts will be needed again – not just against military threats but also to cope with looming ecological catastrophes, disease and hunger. And at this sensitive point, the ambiguity of our stance becomes palpable.

43

In French, the gap between what we say we fear and what we really fear is nicely rendered by the so-called *ne explétif*, a 'no' which doesn't carry any meaning on its own but is used for syntax or pronunciation reasons. (Some other languages like my own, Slovene, also have it.) It mostly occurs in subjunctive subordinate clauses following verbs with negative connotations (*to fear, to avoid, to doubt*); its function is to emphasize the negative aspect of what came before it, as in: '*Elle doute qu'il ne vienne*' (She doubts he's *not* coming') or '*Je te fais confiance à moins que tu ne me mentes*' ('I trust you unless you *don't* lie to me').[49] Jacques Lacan cites *ne explétif* to explain the difference between wish and desire: when I say, 'I am afraid the storm will *not* come,' my conscious wish is that it will not come; I am afraid of the storm. But my true desire is inscribed onto the added 'no' – I am afraid the storm will *not* come. In my heart of hearts, I am fascinated by and desire the violence of a storm.

Does exactly the same not hold for Western Europe's stance towards Ukraine? During the first weeks of the war, we feared Ukraine would be quickly crushed – but now we have to admit that our real fear was exactly the opposite: that Ukraine would not be crushed, that the war would just go on and on. Our secret hope was that Ukraine would quickly fall, so that we could be properly outraged, mourn its loss . . . and then go on with business as usual. What should have been good news – a smaller nation unexpectedly, heroically, resisting a brutal invasion – is something we are almost ashamed of, not knowing what to do with it.

Similarly, we were afraid that the cessation of the flow of Russian gas would cause an economic catastrophe. But what if this fear was a fake, what if we were really afraid to consider the possibility that the interruption of the gas supply would *not* cause a catastrophe (which in the end it didn't)?[50] That we could quickly adapt to it? (This is what is effectively happening now, a year into the war.) Although a sudden end to imports of Russian gas would not have triggered the end of capitalism, it would nonetheless have forced a real shift in the 'European' way of life, a shift that would be most welcome, independently of any aim to constrain Russia. Reading the *ne explétif* literally, acting upon this 'no', is perhaps the main political act of freedom today. Because the alternative is, as Kurt Vonnegut put it, the prospect that 'we'll go down in history as the first society that wouldn't save itself because it wasn't cost effective'?

Our media churn out article after article about the billions that Ukraine is getting from our governments, but (in the first months of the war, at least) Russia was still getting many times more for the gas it delivered to Europe. No wonder that, in Germany, bosses and unions have jointly opposed the boycotting of Russian gas. What Europe has missed is a unique chance to combine *non-military* pressure on Russia with meaningful action for our *environment*. Not to mention the crucial fact that to renounce Russian gas would open up the prospect of a different kind of globalization, one that is needed more than ever today – an order distinct from both Western liberal-capitalism and Russian–Chinese authoritarianism.

The main limitation of the pacifist stance is that it doesn't take into account the fact that the target of Russian aggression is so clearly not only Ukraine but the Western liberal-democratic order as a whole – so we are already well beyond the limited problem of how to contain Russia's attack on Ukraine, the problem on which Habermas has been focused. Russia is aiming to rebuild the world in its image. Yevgeny Prigozhin, formerly one of Putin's strongmen and the big hand behind the Wagner

Group of Russian mercenaries, told a *Guardian* journalist: 'You are a dying-out Western civilization that considers Russians, Malians, Central Africans, Cubans, Nicaraguans and many other peoples and countries to be third world scum. You are a pathetic endangered bunch of perverts, and there are many of us, billions of us. And victory will be ours!'[51] We can get from the Wagner Group's activities an idea of how the new globalization advocated by Russia will look: Russian mercenaries supporting local authoritarian regimes.

I am well aware of the full implications of rejecting the pacifist stance and choosing to support radical, sweeping policies like the boycotting of Russian gas. Measures like this will bring closer the prospect of what I have called 'war communism': whereby our economies and political processes will have to be reorganized in order to cope with the circumstances of war or larger-scale disaster. We have seen glimmers of this already: in the UK, cooking oil was rationed by supermarkets in April 2022 – one could buy two bottles per person maximum. In February 2023, UK supermarkets once again began rationing, though this time with fresh fruit and vegetables – a shortage had been caused by bad weather ruining harvests in North Africa and diminished supplies from European growers hit by soaring energy bills.[52] As the war continues, many more measures of this kind may well become the only way to survive. But Russia counts precisely on Europe's inertia and inability to take such decisive action. Yes, there is a great danger of corruption here, an opportunity for the military-industrial complex to grab super-profits, but this is not just a story about war. I agree that we should resist the temptation of glorifying war as an authentic experience to set against our complacent consumerist hedonism. But our answer to this complacency should be an even stronger mobilization for causes that reach well beyond armed conflicts. With regard to the dangers that confront humanity today, military passion is itself a cowardly escape from the abyss we are gradually approaching.

The multiple crises and apocalyptic prospects we are facing today seem to evoke more and more ominously the four riders of the apocalypse from the Book of Revelations: plague, war, hunger, death.[53] The four riders cannot be simply dismissed as figures of evil – Trevor Hancock has pointed out that they are 'remarkably close to what we might call the four horsemen of ecology that regulate population size in nature.' Referring to Charles Elton, he suggests that the 'four riders' play a positive role in preventing overpopulation: 'increases in numbers are held in check by predators, pathogens, parasites and food supply.' The problem is that, in the long term, this regulatory function didn't seem to work for humans:

> The human population has more than tripled in the past 70 years, from 2.5 billion in 1950 to 7.8 billion today. So what happened to Elton's four ecological horsemen? Why are we not controlled? Is there a fifth horseman that will cause our populations to crash at some point, as lemmings do?

Till recently, humanity was able to hold the four riders in check through medicine, science and technology; now, however, we are threatened by the

> massive and rapid global ecological changes we have triggered. So although of course an asteroid strike or super-volcano eruption could wipe us out, the greatest threat to the human population, the 'fifth horseman' if you like, is us.'[54]

What this means is that we – humanity – are now facing a key decision: we can either cause our own destruction or save ourselves from it. Although global awareness of this threat is growing, it is not followed by adequate activity, while the other four riders are galloping faster and faster:

Plague has become part of our lives again. At the end of 2019, Covid appeared and changed our lives forever – it is still here and we can expect new waves, as well as other viral pandemics.

War With the Russian attack on Ukraine, we got a true hot war in Europe – a sobering reminder that nobody can afford to observe war from a safe distance. Even if some kind of truce is enforced, war has forcefully reasserted itself as a general condition of our lives, showing peace to be a temporary exception. Whichever way we turn, the Third World War is on the horizon, and what is needed is not just or even primarily the strength to counter the aggressors but a radical change of the entire global system. As we have seen, the situation is open: if there is a new global war, it will retroactively appear to have been necessary, so we should be aware that we should be acting against the trend of history (which tends towards our self-destruction). A minor proposal: anyone who publicly declares that he is ready to use nuclear weapons should be treated as an obscene freak.

Hunger is also on the horizon. The War in Ukraine has created the greatest global food crisis since the Second World War, and experts are warning that it could lead to food riots in poor nations.[55] Because of global warming, heatwaves in India and Pakistan are 'testing the limits of human survivability', with massive crops failures there.[56] Are we getting ready for the mass migrations and riots that global hunger will trigger?

Death is in itself always part of life. Suffice it to recall a deeply true Polish graffiti definition of life as a sexually transmitted disease that always ends in death. But what I mean when I say that death is the fourth rider is something more radical; I am not just referring to the excessive deaths caused by the other three riders. It is our 'second death' through the latest modes of the digital control of our daily lives, especially the prospect of the 'wired brain' (the direct link of our minds with digital machines) – will we still be human, and in what sense, if this happens?

So what can we do? The Grass Mud Horse, or Caonima, is a Chinese internet meme based on a pun: it is a word play on the Mandarin words *cào nǐ mā*, literally, 'fuck your mother'. Caonima is an exemplary case of the 'resistance discourse' of Chinese internet users, a mascot of netizens in China fighting for free expression, inspiring poetry, photos and videos, artwork, lines of clothing, and more. As such, it is part of a broader Chinese internet culture of spoofing, mockery, punning and parody known as *e'gao*, which includes video mash-ups and other types of bricolage.[57] Here we can see how concrete freedom, which resides in following the established rules of language, also needs moments of abstract freedom (freely playing with these rules) to be really alive in a language. Far from being a purist dream of respecting others, actual global solidarity cannot survive without mockery and punning.

The Safari State of Mind

I don't like to write about cultural products from my own country, but I simply have to make an exception for *Sarajevo Safari* by Miran Zupanič (Slovenia, 2022), a documentary about arguably the most bizarre pathological event that took place during the siege of Sarajevo from 1992 to 1996. It is well known that snipers on the hills surrounding Sarajevo occupied by Serb forces were shooting random residents on the streets below them. It was also well known that selected Serb allies (mostly Russians) were invited to have a couple of shots on Sarajevo, but this was considered an honour, a sign of special appreciation, not a matter of business. With Zupanič's film, however, we have now learned about the real business on those hills. Dozens of rich foreigners (mostly from the US, UK and Italy, although some were also from Russia) paid high fees for the chance to shoot at the residents of besieged Sarajevo. The trip was organized by the Bosnian Serb Army: the customers were transported from Belgrade to Pale (the capital of Serbian Bosnia in the mountains near Sarajevo) and then brought to a safe place with a view of Sarajevo down the valley.[58]

We learn from the documentary that not only the high command of the Serb Bosnian Army but also NATO peacekeeping forces in Bosnia were aware of this safari. So why didn't they render it public or simply bomb the sniper station? But what is of special interest here is the subjectivity of a safari 'hunter'. Their victims were not personalized, they remained anonymous; a symbolic wall separated the hunter from the target. It was, none-theless, not a video game: these victims were living, breathing humans, and the hunter's awareness of this fact accounts for the perverse thrill of such 'hunting'. To be more precise, it is not the victim who was here de-realized, it was the hunter himself. It was the hunter, not the victim, who excluded himself from ordinary reality and perceived himself as being located in some safe place above the real world. In this way, reality itself was made part of a spectacle in which the hunter could pretend that he was not personally involved.

There is something perversely honest in all of this: are today's top corporate managers not engaged in a similar safari? Their decisions may ruin many lives, and thousands may lose their jobs at their hands – and we can imagine some of them observing the ruined families of the employees they've fired or otherwise humiliated. And – our final example of the same madness – did Dmitry Medvedev, the former Russian president who now serves as deputy chairman of Russia's Security Council, not rely on a similar logic when he asserted that 'the US-led NATO military alliance would be too scared of a "nuclear apocalypse"' to directly enter the conflict in response to Russia deploying tactical nuclear weapons:

> I believe that NATO will not directly intervene in the conflict even in this situation. After all, the security of Washington, London, Brussels is much more important for the North Atlantic Alliance than the fate of a dying Ukraine that no one needs . . . The supply of modern weapons is just a business for Western countries. Overseas and European demagogues are not going to perish in a nuclear apocalypse. Therefore, they will swallow the use of any weapon in the current conflict.[59]

Are we aware what these sentences imply? Medvedev is ready to risk the lives of billions for a small piece of land – billions in Latin America, Africa and Asia who are not involved in the Ukrainian conflict. Back in August 2022, Medvedev said that a proposal to punish Russia for war crimes in Ukraine threatened the existence of mankind, given Moscow's nuclear arsenal.[60] Again, what vantage point does Medvedev speak from when he talks like that? What is his subjective position? He does not include himself among those who will perish; he talks as if somehow he will survive the global nuclear catastrophe – as if humanity is, like Sarajevo, in a valley and he is at a safe distance on a hill above it. Of course he knows that he will be affected by the end of mankind, but he speaks as if he doesn't.

It is clear to everybody that Medvedev's words have to be read against the background of Russia's formal annexation of parts of Ukraine: in this way, any Ukrainian intrusion into those parts could be declared a threat to the survival of Russia as a state, and thus justify the use of tactical nuclear weapons. Not being a specialist, I am going to put to one side the wider context of this move (Russian military setbacks, and so on); I just want to follow Medvedev's logic to the end. He also said Russia will 'do every-thing' to prevent nuclear weapons from appearing in 'our hostile neighbors' like 'Nazi Ukraine' – but since it is Russia that is threatening the very existence of another state (Ukraine), does this other state not also have the right to defend its existence by tactical nuclear weapons? We should thus take seriously the idea that Ukraine should be given nuclear weapons to establish a basic parity with Russia. Recall Putin's words in June 2022:

In order to claim some kind of leadership – I am not even talk-ing about global leadership, I mean leadership in any area – any country, any people, any ethnic group should ensure their sovereignty. Because there is no in-between, no intermediate state: either a country is sovereign, or it is a colony, no matter what the colonies are called.[61]

From these lines it is clear that, in Putin's view, Ukraine falls into the latter category: it is a colony, no matter what it is called. Our strategy should be to treat Ukraine as no one's colony – ourselves included. This is also why we should resolutely reject Harlan Ullman's argument that, in the same way peace in Korea was achieved by direct negotiations between the US and the opposite side, bypassing South Korea, powerful Western states should also intervene directly in negotiations with Russia, bypassing Ukraine:

How does this war end if Putin is determined to win? Should we not be at least considering acceptable terms for all parties to end the war? Clemenceau observed that 'war is too important to be left to the generals.' In this case, is Ukraine too important to be left to Zelensky? The United States needs a strategy with an off-ramp to seek an end to the violence and the war.[62]

But is this not precisely what Russia wants? I have no doubt that some Leftist peaceniks will react to my suggestion with horror, interpreting statements like Medvedev's as a serious warning to Ukraine and the West to show restraint – we shouldn't, they'd cry, push Russia too far into a corner. This, however, is precisely the stance we must avoid at any price. The peaceniks who are against NATO and sending arms to Ukraine ignore the key fact that *it was Western help that allowed Ukraine to resist at all* – without it, all of Ukraine would be long occupied. This help led to the stalemate we are currently in; it created the conditions for possible peace talks (although as we know, the situation can escalate again at any moment). The peaceniks, from Chomsky through Varoufakis to Peterson, are the most despicable figures in our public space today: they first insisted that Ukraine simply could not win a war against Russia, but when it began to appear to win, they started asserting that it shouldn't (or shouldn't be allowed to) win (or even gain too much ground), because this might provoke Putin's ire, prompting him to push the button. In this vision, Putin is not a ruthless conqueror but a dangerous madman, so peace (the prevention of nuclear war) should have priority over all other considerations.

For many months, the West has been obsessed by what is going on in Putin's mind (although to me his goals are pretty clear). I think what is much more enigmatic and ambiguous is what goes on in the Western liberal mind. Recall how, in the first days of the war, Western powers offered to get Zelensky out of Kyiv on a special plane, implying that the situation was already lost (so let's get out of here fast). This hysterical, precipitous offer made palpable the true desire of the West – a desire that was spoiled by the unexpected success of Ukrainian resistance. We hear again and again that Russia should be allowed to save face – but statements like Medvedev's make it impossible for Ukraine and the West to save *their* faces, declaring in advance that compromise would be proof of Western cowardice! So, yes, some form of negotiated compromise will probably be necessary, but this compromise should pay no attention to the question of saving the face of Russia in the sense of again recognizing it as a 'normal' state and returning to economic and cultural relations as if the war had never happened. Russia should be treated as what it is, a very dangerous failed state. But why, then, is Medvedev publicly saying what he is saying? Why does he add insult to injury and in advance interpret the Western refusal to respond with a nuclear counterattack as a sign of timidity? Is the only interpretation not this: Russia is making a negotiated resolution to the conflict as difficult as possible, and it is doing this because it is acting with safari subjectivity.

But the true madness resides in the fact that we are talking about the threat of nuclear annihilation while we are all committing collective suicide by way of ignoring ongoing environmental changes – as if the self-annihilation towards which we are already slowly drifting can be made less terrifying if we focus on the potential future of nuclear war. This threat of nuclear destruction makes us (not all of us, but those who can push the buttons) a version of *homo deus*, but in a negative sense: the only divine act we are now able to commit is that of self-destruction – something that, as we learned recently, a stupid virus is also able to do.

This brings us back to our starting point: the situation described in *Sarajevo Safari* is increasingly becoming the basic situation of the privileged elite not just in the West but in all parts of the world. We don't live *in* the real world, reality is in the valley that we observe from a safe distance, and we intervene in it for a thrilling experience that does not endanger us. Unfortunately, reality catches up with us from time to time, and we mostly react to it like the peace-loving West, trying not to provoke the beast in the valley too much, oblivious to its insatiable rage.

I am reminded here of John Lennon's mega-hit 'Imagine', which was for me always a fake song, a song that became popular for the wrong reasons. Imagining that the world could, eventually, 'live as one' is the best way to end up in hell. Those who have clung to pacifism in the face of the Russian attack on Ukraine remain caught in their own version of 'imagine' – imagine a post-heroic world in which tensions are no longer resolved through armed conflicts . . . Europe has persisted in this imagined world, ignoring the brutal reality beyond its borders. But the dream of a quick Ukrainian victory, which was really just a repetition of the initial dream of a quick Russian victory, was over many months ago. As time has passed, the situation has become clearer and clearer; and there is no longer any need to read between the lines when Putin compares himself with Peter the Great:

> On the face of it, he was at war with Sweden, taking something away from it . . . He was not taking away anything, he was returning . . . He was returning and reinforcing, that is what he was doing . . . Clearly, it fell to our lot to return and reinforce as well.[63]

Recall Putin's claim that: 'there are two categories of state: The sovereign and the conquered.' In his imperial view, Ukraine should fall into the latter category.[64] And, as is no less clear from Russian official statements in recent months, so do Bosnia and Herzegovina, Kosovo, Finland, the Baltic states . . . and ultimately Europe itself. So Western pacifists are asking us to accept not a minor territorial compromise in Donbas but Putin's imperial ambition as a whole. The reason this ambition should be unconditionally rejected is that in today's global world, in which we are all haunted by the same catastrophes, we are *all* in-between, in an intermediate state, neither a sovereign country nor a conquered one. To insist on full sovereignty in the face of global warming is sheer madness, since our very survival hinges on tight global cooperation.

But Russia isn't simply ignoring climate change. Why was it so mad at the Scandinavian countries when they expressed their intention of joining NATO? With global warming, what is at stake is the control of the Arctic passage (thats why Trump wanted to buy Greenland from Denmark). Due to the explosive economic development of China, Japan and South Korea, the main transport routes of the future will run north of Russia and Scandinavia. Russia's strategic plan is to *profit* from global warming: control the world's main transport route, in addition to developing Siberia and controlling Ukraine. In this way, Russia will dominate so much of the global food production and supply chain that it will be able to blackmail the whole world. This is the ultimate economic reality beneath Putin's imperial dream.

Those who have advocated putting more pressure on Ukraine to negotiate, inclusive of accepting painful territorial losses, like to repeat that Ukraine simply cannot win the war against Russia – to think so is madness. True, but I see exactly in this the greatness of Ukrainian resistance: they risked the impossible, defying pragmatic calculations, and the least we owe them is full support, and to do this, we need a stronger NATO – but not as a prolongation of existing US politics. The US strategy to counteract Russian geopolitical might through machinations in Europe is self-evident: not just Ukraine, Europe as a whole is becoming the site of a proxy war between the US and Russia, which may well conclude with a compromise between the two at Europe's expense. There are only two options available to Europe: to play the game of neutrality – a short-cut to catastrophe – or to become an autonomous agent. (Just think how the situation may change if DeSantis or Trump wins the 2024 US elections.)

While some Leftists claim that the ongoing war is in the interest of the NATO military-industrial complex, which uses the need for new arms as a means of avoiding internal crisis and gaining profits, their true message to Ukraine is: OK, you are victims of brutal aggression, but do not rely on our arms because in this way you are playing into the hands of a military-industrial complex ... The disorientation caused by the Ukrainian war is producing strange bedfellows like Henry Kissinger and Noam Chomsky, who both argue that Ukraine should consider a settlement that could see it surrendering some of its territory to achieve a quicker peace deal.[65]

This version of 'pacifism' only works if we neglect the key fact that the war is not about Ukraine but a moment in a brutal attempt to change our entire geopolitical situation. The true target of the war is the dismantlement of the European unity advocated not only by the US conservatives and Russia but also by the European extreme Right and Left – at this point, in France, Melenchon meets Le Pen.

What is absolutely unacceptable for a true Leftist today is not only to support Russia but also to make a more 'modest' neutral claim that the Left is divided between pacifists and supporters of Ukraine, and that one should treat this division as a minor fact that shouldn't affect the Left's global struggle against global capitalism – why? Remember Mao Zedong's distinction between 'principal' and 'secondary' contradictions (the 'struggle between opposites'), set out in his 1937 treatise *On Contradiction* – perhaps this distinction deserves to be brought back to life. A contradiction, a struggle, is never single, it depends on other contradiction(s). Here is Mao's own example: in a capitalist society, the 'principal' contradiction between the proletariat and the bourgeoisie is accompanied by other 'secondary' contradictions, such as the one between imperialists and their colonies. While these secondary contradictions depend on the first one (for colonies exist only in capitalism), the principal contradiction is not always the dominant one: contradictions can trade places of importance. Say, when a country is occupied, it is the ruling class that is usually bribed to collaborate with the occupiers to maintain its privileged position, turning the struggle against the occupiers into the priority. The same can go for the struggle against racism: in a state of racial tension and exploitation, the only way to effectively struggle for the working class is to focus on fighting racism (this is why any appeal to the white working class, as in today's alt-right populist world, is a betrayal of class struggle).

Today, the struggle for Ukraine's freedom is the 'dominant' contradiction: you *cannot* be a Leftist if you do not unequivocally stand behind Ukraine. To be a Leftist who 'shows understanding' for Russia is like being one of those Leftists who, before Germany attacked the USSR, took seriously the German 'anti-imperialist' rhetoric directed at the UK and so advocated neutrality in Germany's war against France. If the Left fails at this stage, it's game over. But does this mean that the Left should simply take the side of the West, alongside those Rightist fundamentalists who also support the Ukrainian struggle?

In a speech in Dallas in May 2022, while criticizing Russia's political system, the ex-president Bush said: 'The result is an absence of checks and balances in Russia, and the decision of one man to launch a wholly unjustified and brutal invasion of Iraq.' He quickly corrected himself: 'I mean, of Ukraine,' then said 'Iraq, anyway,' to laughter from the crowd, and added 'seventy-five', referring to his age.[66] As many commentators noted, two things cannot but strike the eye in this rather obvious Freudian slip: the fact that the public received Bush's implicit confession that the US attack on Iraq (ordered by him) was 'a wholly unjustified and brutal invasion' with laughter, instead of treating it as an admission of a crime comparable to the Russian invasion of Ukraine; plus Bush's enigmatic continuation of his self-correction – 'Iraq, anyway' – what did he mean by that? That the difference between Ukraine and Iraq doesn't really matter? The final reference to his advanced age does nothing to resolve the enigma in any way. It is, however, dispelled completely the moment we take Bush's statement seriously and literally. Yes, with all differences taken into account (Zelensky is not, for example, a dictator like Saddam), Bush did the very same thing that Putin is now doing to Ukraine, so they should both be judged by the same standard.

But they are not. On 17 June 2022, we learned from the media that WikiLeaks founder Julian Assange's extradition to the US was approved by the UK Home Secretary, Priti Patel. His crime? Nothing other than to render public the crimes confessed by Bush's slip of tongue: the documents revealed by WikiLeaks revealed how, under Bush's presidency, 'the US military had killed hundreds of civilians in unreported incidents during the war in Afghanistan, while leaked Iraq war files showed 66,000 civilians had been killed, and prisoners tortured'[67] – crimes fully comparable with what Putin is doing in Ukraine. With hindsight, we can now say that WikiLeaks disclosed dozens of American Buchas and Mariupols. So while putting Bush on trial is no less illusory than bringing Putin to the Hague tribunal, the minimum to be done by those who oppose the Russian invasion of Ukraine would be to demand Assange's immediate release.

Ukraine claims it fights for Europe, and Russia claims it fights for the rest of the world against Western unipolar hegemony. Both claims should be rejected, and here the difference between Right and Left enters the stage. From the Rightist standpoint, Ukraine fights for European values against the non-European authoritarians; from the Leftist standpoint, Ukraine fights for global freedom, inclusive of the freedom of Russians themselves. That's why the heart of every true Russian patriot beats for Ukraine. And, much more importantly, that's why we should stop being obsessed with the topic of

'What goes on in Putin's mind?' – do the people around him tell him the whole truth? Is he ill or insane? Are we pushing him into a corner where he will see no other way out to save his face than to accelerate the conflict into a total war? We should stop this obsession with the red line, this endless search for the right measure between support for Ukraine and avoiding total war. The 'red line' is not an objective fact: Putin himself is redrawing it all the time, and we contribute to his redrawing with our reactions. A question like 'Did US intelligence-sharing with Ukraine cross a line?'[68] makes us obliterate the basic fact: it was Russia itself which crossed the line with the attack on Ukraine. So instead of perceiving ourselves as a group that just reacts to Putin as an impenetrable evil genius, we should turn the gaze back at ourselves: what do we – the 'free West' – want in this affair?

We should analyse the ambiguity of our support for Ukraine with the same scrutiny with which we analyse Russia's stance. We should reach beyond the double standards applied today to the very foundations of European liberalism. Remember how, in the Western liberal tradition, colonization was often justified in the terms of the rights of working people. John Locke, the great Enlightenment philosopher and advocate of human rights, justified the fact that white settlers were grabbing land from native Americans with a strange Left-sounding argument against excessive private property. His premise was that an individual should be allowed to own only as much land as he is able to use productively, not large tracts of land that he is not able to use (and then eventually gives to others to use and gains rent from it). In North America, the natives claimed that the vast tracts of land were theirs although they were not using them productively, mostly just for hunting of non-domesticated animals, so their land was wasted and the white settlers who wanted to use it for agriculture had the right to seize it for the benefit of humanity . . .

In the ongoing crisis, both sides continually present themselves as having been obligated to take action: the West has to help Ukraine remain free and independent, Russia is compelled to intervene militarily to protect its safety. Here's one example: the Kremlin would be 'forced to take retaliatory steps' if Finland's bid to join NATO succeeded, according to the Russian Foreign Ministry in 2022[69] – but no, it will not be 'forced', in the same way that Russia was not 'forced' to attack Ukraine. This decision appears as 'forced' only if you accept the whole suite of ideological and geopolitical assumptions that sustain Russian politics. These assumptions have to be analysed closely, without any taboos. One often hears that we should draw a strict line of separation between Putin's politics and Russian culture as a whole, but this line is much more porous than it may appear. We should resolutely reject the idea that, after years of patiently trying to resolve the Ukrainian crisis through negotiations, Russia was finally compelled to attack Ukraine – one is never forced to attack and annihilate a whole country. The roots are much deeper; I am ready to call them properly metaphysical. Anatoly Chubais, the father of Russian oligarchs (who orchestrated the rapid privatization of state industries in 1992), said in 2004:

> I've re-read all of Dostoevsky over the past three months. And I feel nothing but almost physical hatred for the man. He is certainly a genius, but his idea of Russians as special, holy people, his cult of suffering and the false choices he presents make me want to tear him to pieces.[70]

As much as I dislike Chubais for his politics, I think he was right about Dostoyevsky, who provided the 'deepest' expression of the opposition between Europe and Russia: individualism versus collective spirit, materialist hedonism versus the spirit of sacrifice . . .

In step with Dostoevsky, Russia has presented its invasion as a new stage in the fight for decolonization, against Western globalization. The world is, according to Medvedev, 'waiting for the collapse of the idea of an American-centric world and the emergence of new international alliances based on pragmatic criteria.' ('Pragmatic criteria' means disregard for universal human rights, of course.) But I agree with Medvedev when he attributes to the West 'complete disregard for the right to private property, which until recent events was one of the pillars of Western democracy' – yes, we will have to limit the 'right to private property', not just of Russian oligarchs but also of our home-grown neo-feudal billionaires!

So we should also start drawing red lines, but crucially we must do so in a way that makes clear our solidarity with the Third World. Medvedev predicted that, because of the war in Ukraine, 'in some states, hunger may occur due to the food crisis'[71] – a statement of breathtaking cynicism, given that, in May 2022, when he made the statement, around 25 million tonnes of grain were slowly rotting in Odessa, on ships or in silos, since the port was blocked by the Russian navy. The Black Sea Grain Initiative, signed in July 2022, allowed the ports to reopen, but, months later, the rate of ships leaving still remained critically low, and in July 2023 the deal collapsed.[72] Beyond making promises to help Ukraine to transport the grain by railway and in trucks, Europe has not done enough, leaving 'fifty million people knocking on famine's door', according to WFP director David Beasley. A step more is needed: we must demand that the ports are fully opened, inclusive of sending military ships to protect them. This is not just about Ukraine, it's about the hunger of hundreds of millions in Africa and Asia. This is where the red line should be drawn.

In the early months of the conflict, Lavrov said: 'Imagine [that the Ukraine war] is happening in Africa, or the Middle East. Imagine Ukraine is Palestine. Imagine Russia is the United States.'[73] As expected, comparing the conflict in Ukraine with the plight of the Palestinians 'offended many Israelis, who believe there are no similarities. For example, many point out that Ukraine is a sovereign, democratic country, but don't consider Palestine as a state,' *Newsweek* reported.[74] Of course Palestine is not a state, *because Israel denies its right to be a state* – in the same way Russia denies Ukraine's right to be a sovereign state. As much as I find Lavrov's remarks repulsive – he sometimes deftly manipulates the truth – the least one can say is that his 'imagine' is much more thought-provoking than Lennon's.

Yes, the liberal West is hypocritical, applying its high standards very selectively. But hypocrisy means you violate the standards you proclaim, and in this way you open yourself up to immanent criticism: when we criticize the liberal West, we use its own standards. What Russia is offering is a world without hypocrisy – because it is without global ethical standards, practising just pragmatic 'respect' for difference. We were given an unmistakeable demonstration of what this means when, after the Taliban took over in Afghanistan, they instantly made a deal with China: China accepted the new Afghanistan regime, while the Taliban agreed to ignore what China is doing to the Uyghurs – this is, *in nuce*, the new globalization advocated by Russia. And the only way to defend what is worth saving in our liberal tradition is to ruthlessly insist on its universality – the moment we apply double standards, we are no less 'pragmatic' than Russia. Universality means here that there is no place for 'Safari' subjectivity: we are part of reality, not residing above it.

What About the Rest of the World?

After the Russian invasion of Ukraine began, I was yet again ashamed of being a citizen of Slovenia. The Slovene government immediately proclaimed that it was ready to receive thousands of Ukrainian refugees fleeing Russian occupation. That might seem reasonable, but when Afghanistan fell to the Taliban six months earlier, this same government announced that Slovenia was not ready to receive any refugees from there – the justification being that, instead of escaping, people should stay and fight the Taliban with guns. Along the same lines, when thousands of refugees from Asia tried to enter Poland from Belarus in July 2021, the Slovene government offered Poland military help, claiming that Europe was under attack. So there are obviously two categories of refugee, 'ours' (European), i.e. 'real' refugees, and the Third World ones who don't deserve our hospitality. The Slovene government posted a tweet the day after the Russian invasion making this distinction clear: 'The refugees from Ukraine are coming from an environment which is in its cultural, religious, and historical sense something totally different from the environment out of which refugees from Afghanistan are coming.' After the outcry this tweet provoked, it was soon withdrawn – but the genie of the obscene truth left the bottle for a brief moment.

I don't mention this so much for moral reasons – though the moral issue is undeniable – but because I think such a 'defence of Europe' will be catastrophic for Western Europe in the ongoing global struggle for geopolitical influence. Our media are now focused on the conflict between the Western 'liberal' sphere and the Russian 'Eurasian' sphere, each side accusing the other of posing an existential threat: the West, according to Russia, is fomenting 'colour revolutions' in the East (not only in Ukraine but also in Belarus, Moldova, Bulgaria . . .) with the aim of encircling Russia with NATO states; meanwhile, Russia brutally tries to restore its control over the entire ex-Soviet domain, and nobody knows where it will stop. It has already made it clear that it will not just stand and observe if Bosnia and Herzegovina gets closer to NATO (which probably means it will support the secession of the Serb region of Bosnia). All of this is part of a larger geopolitical game, though – just recall the Russian military presence in Syria which saved the Assad regime.

What the West largely ignores is the third much larger group of countries that mostly just observe the conflict: the rest of the world, from Latin America to the Middle East, from Africa to South-East Asia. Even China is not ready to fully support Russia, although it has its own plans to use the conflict to its advantage. At the start of the invasion, in a message to Kim Jong Un, Xi Jinping said China was ready to work together with the Korean side, to steadily develop the China–DPRK relations of friendship and cooperation 'under a new situation'[75] – a coded reference to the Ukrainian war – and there remains a fear that China will use this 'new situation' to 'liberate' Taiwan.

This is why it is not enough just to repeat the obvious. Right from the beginning, Putin told us all we needed to know about the Russian position. The day after the invasion, Putin called on the Ukrainian military to seize power in their country and overthrow President Zelensky, claiming it would be 'easier for us to come to an agreement [with you]' than with 'this gang of drug addicts and neo-Nazis [the Ukrainian government]' who have 'taken the entire Ukrainian people hostage'.[76] We should also note how Russia has immediately militarized any and every counter-measure: when Western states began to consider excluding Russia from SWIFT (the intermediary for financial transactions), Russia replied that this would equal an act of war – as if they had not already started a large-scale actual war? When he announced the invasion, Putin made this clear: 'To anyone who would consider interfering from the outside – if you do, you will face consequences greater than any you have faced in history.'[77] Let's just try to take this statement seriously: 'interfering from the outside' can mean a lot of things, including sending defensive military equipment to Ukraine; 'consequences greater than any you have faced in history'? European countries have faced two world wars with millions dead, so a 'greater' consequence can only be nuclear destruction.

Those who urge 'understanding' for Russian military acts are, as we've seen, a group of strange bed-fellows. Perhaps the saddest part of the story is that quite a few on the liberal Left thought the crisis was just a game of bluffing, since both sides knew they could not afford a full war – their message was: 'Just take it easy, don't lose your nerve, and nothing will happen.' And some others on the 'Left' (I cannot use the word here without quote marks) have actually gone so far as to place the blame on the West – parroting the Russian line that NATO was slowly strangling and destabilizing Russia, encircling it militarily, ignoring Russia's quite reasonable fears; after all, Russia was twice attacked from the West in the last century . . . There is, of course, an element of truth in this, but this reasoning is the same as justifying Hitler's regime on the basis that the unjust Versailles treaty crushed the German economy. It also implies that the big powers have the right to control their own spheres of influence, sacrificing the autonomy of small nations on the altar of global stability. Putin repeatedly claimed that he was forced to intervene militarily since there was no other choice – in its own way this is true, but we have to raise the key question here: military intervention appears as Putin's TINA ('there is no alternative') *only if we accept in advance his global vision of politics as the struggle of big powers to defend and expand their sphere of influence.*

So what about Putin's accusations of Ukrainian Fascism? We should rather turn the question around and direct it at Putin himself: all those who have any illusions about Putin should note the fact that he elevated to the status of his official phil-osopher Ivan Ilyin, a Russian political theologist who, after being expelled from the Soviet Union in the early 1920s on the famous 'philosophers' steamboat', advocated, against both Bolshevism and Western liberalism, his version of Russian Fas-cism: the state as an organic community led by a paternal monarch. For Ilyin, the social system is like a body; each of us has a place in this body, and freedom means knowing your place. Accordingly, for Ilyin, democracy is a ritual: 'We only vote in order to affirm our collective support for our leader. The leader is not legitimated by our votes or chosen by our votes.'[78] Is this not how Russian elections have *de facto* operated in the last few decades? No wonder Ilyin's works are now mas-sively reprinted in Russia, with free copies given to state apparatchiks and military conscripts. Aleksander Dugin, Putin's postmodern court-philosopher, closely follows in Ilyin's steps, just adding a post-modern spin of historicist relativism:

Post-modernity shows that every so-called truth is a matter of believing. So we believe in what we do, we believe in what we say. And that is the only way to define the truth. So we have our special Russian truth that you need to accept. If the United States does not want to start a war, you should recognize that United States is not any more a unique master. And [with] the situation in Syria and Ukraine, Russia says, 'No, you are not any more the boss.' That is the question of who rules the world. Only war could decide really.[79]

The immediate question here is: but what about the people of Syria, of the Central African Republic, of Ukraine? Can they also choose their truth/belief or are they just a playground of the big 'bosses' and their struggle? The idea that each 'way of life' has its own 'truth' is what makes Putin so popular among the new populist Right – no wonder his military intervention in Ukraine was greeted by Trump and others as the act of a 'genius'.[80] So when Putin talks about 'denazification', we should just remember that this is the same Putin who supported Marine le Pen in France, Lega in Italy, and other *actual* neo-Fascist movements.

But there is nothing surprising in any of this. Forget about 'Russian truth'; this is just a convenient myth to justify one's power. So, to really counter Putin, we should build bridges to the rest of the world – to those countries beyond Europe's borders, many of whom have a long list of fully justified grievances against Western colonization and exploitation. It's not enough just to 'defend Europe': our true task is to convince the countries of the Third World, in the face of our global challenges, we can offer them a better choice than Russia or China. We must convince them with action: putting an end to our ongoing ecological and economic neo-colonialist exploitation, easing the burden of debt, resolving crises which cause mass emigration, establishing worldwide healthcare coordination, so that grossly unfair practices like vaccine hoarding cease to occur. The only way to achieve this is to change *ourselves* – to go well beyond Politically Correct post-colonialism and ruthlessly extirpate forms of neo-colonialism even when they are masked as humanitarian help.

If we don't, we will just be left to wonder why many in the Third World don't see that, in defending Europe, we are fighting also for their freedom – they don't see it because we are not really doing it. The fate of Assange is a clear sign of how our hypocrisy prevails, so no wonder that, though Russia may not be gaining ground in Ukraine, it is gaining credibility in the Global South. In early 2023, Luiz Inácio Lula da Silva, the newly re-elected President of Brasil, said that Zelensky and Putin bear equal responsibility for the war in Ukraine, thereby joining the club of 'neutral' countries, like South Africa and India, whose neutrality is strictly pro-Russian. Neutrality is here the neutrality of somebody walking down a street, seeing a child being beaten by a much bigger, stronger man, and calmly walking past the terrible scene, retorting to the desperate cries for help: 'Sorry, I am neutral!'

At around the same time, the English musician Roger Waters addressed the UN Security Council through a video call and said he was representing 'the feelings of countless brothers and sisters all over the world' when he said:

> The invasion of Ukraine by the Russian Federation was illegal. I condemn it in the strongest possible terms. Also, the Russian invasion of Ukraine was not unprovoked. So I also condemn the provocateurs in the strongest possible terms . . . the only sensible course of action today is to call for an immediate ceasefire in Ukraine, no ifs, no buts, no ands. Not one more

Ukrainian or Russian life is to be spent, not one, they are all precious in our eyes. So the time has come to speak truth to power.'

But is this actual neutrality? To which power does Waters want to 'speak truth'? In an interview with the *Berliner Zeitung* he said: 'I am now more open to listen to what Putin actually says. According to independent voices I listen to, he governs carefully, making decisions on the grounds of a consensus in the Russian Federation government.'[81]

Is this what we learn when we listen to what Putin 'actually says'? I am closely following Russian media, and I see regularly on its big TV channels debates in which participants argue that Russia should nuke Poland, Germany, the UK. I hear and read 'argumentation' that describes the Russian attack on Ukraine as a struggle for de-nazification and de-demonization, making it sound as if the ultimate target were the LGBT+ rights movement's undermining of traditional forms of sexuality (one of the reproaches to Ukraine was that it allowed Pride parades). You repeatedly hear surprising expressions like 'liberal totalitarianism' – one commentator went so far as to claim that Orwell's *1984* was a critique not of Fascism or Stalinism but of liberalism. Putin's ally Kadyrev stated that, after Ukraine, Russsia should go on to 'denazify and demilitarize the next country . . . the fight against Satanism should continue throughout Europe and, first of all, on the territory of Poland.'[82]

But what I don't find are similar statements in the Western media: in spite of all possible exaggerations, their main mantra is that we should help Ukraine to survive. As far as I know, nobody is demanding that Russia's borders should be changed, that a chunk of Russian territory should be taken by other states. This line of reasoning should be followed to the end:

demands to boycott Russian culture are also extremely counter-productive since they *de facto* elevate the Putin regime into a defender of Pushkin, Tchaikovsky and Tolstoy. We should on the contrary insist that we are defending the great Russian tradition against its abusers. And we should avoid triumphalism – we should not demand that Russia should be humiliated. Our goal should remain positive: not 'Russia must lose!' but 'Ukraine must survive!'

The standard argument made by the 'neutral' countries throughout the rest of the world is that, in Ukraine, we are dealing with a local conflict that pales compared to colonial horrors, or to more recent events like the US occupation of Iraq. This argument misses the point: with the Russian attack on Ukraine, we have a brutal colonial war in Europe itself, and solidarity should be with the colonized. Those states who choose to play neutrality forfeit the right to complain about the horrors of colonization anywhere. It's the same with the Palestinian conflict: if you really want to fight anti-Semitism, you also have to support Palestinian resistance to what Israel is doing on the West Bank.

It's as simple as that, and sometimes things *are* as simple as that. Especially now, over a year into the war, when Russia has celebrated the anniversary of its attack with new destructive offensives, it is obscene to blame Ukraine, to disqualify their heroic resistance as a rejection of peace. The more aggressive Russia gets, the more pressure 'neutralists' around the world are putting on Ukraine to abandon its self-defence. Since these neutralists keep ignoring the obvious, we have to keep saying it, however boring it gets to repeat the same warnings again and again. The signs clearly indicate, now as they did at the start of the war, that Russia intends to keep fighting until the

West gets fed up and pressures Kyiv into appeasing them with whatever territory they have taken by then – this is what Russia's 'peace initiatives' are all about.

The only way to keep open a chance of peace in such a situation is to accept that we already live in an emergency state and act accordingly. Yes, Waters is right, Ukraine is 'provoking' Russia – it is provoking Russia's imperial ambitions by way of resisting even when the situation is desperate. Today, not provoking Russia means surrender.

Against the Solidarity of Those in Power

Recall the well-known answer of the members of an Aboriginal tribe to the explorer who visits them for the first time and asks, 'Are there still cannibals among you? Are you a cannibal?'

'No, we're not cannibals, we ate the last one yesterday.'

If a civilized non-cannibal community is constituted by its members eating the last cannibal, that community could never be constituted if that 'last' act of cannibalism were labelled as such, as a criminal act of cannibalism – so it is erased from memory and proclaimed sacred.

Similarly, the passage from 'barbarism' to the modern legal order in the 'Wild West' of the US was accomplished through brutal crimes, through eating the last cannibals, and legends were invented to obfuscate them – this is what John Ford aimed at in his famous line: 'When the legend becomes fact, print the legend.' Legend 'becomes fact' not in the simple sense of factual truth but in the sense that it becomes an immanent constituent of the actually existing socio-political order, so that rejecting it amounts to the disintegration of this order.

And such illegal practices go on continuously. Modern extra-legal practices, supported and enabled by the legally existing apparatuses of power – like torture euphemistically called 'enhanced interrogation techniques' – bear witness to the fact that our states have continued to rely on the dark side, on brutality that is made visible to us only by whistleblowers.

Today, however, something much stranger is happening. A new type of political leader is emerging who – to quote from Alenka Zupančič's *Let Them Rot* –

take[s] pride in committing [a] crime openly rather than secretly, as if it amounted to some kind of fundamental moral difference or difference of character, namely, 'having the courage,' 'the guts,' to do it openly. But what may appear to be their courageous transgression of state laws by avoiding the 'hypocrisy' that those laws sometimes demand is nothing more than a direct identification with the obscene other side of state power itself. It does not amount to anything else or different. They are 'transgressing' their own laws. This is why, even when they are in power, these leaders continue to act as if they are in opposition to the existing power, rebelling against it – call it the 'deep state' or something else.[83]

The unsurpassed model of the obscene leader publicly violating the law is, of course, Donald Trump. In March 2022, Trump called for the Constitution to be terminated, in order to overturn the results of the 2020 election and reinstate himself as President: 'Do you throw the Presidential Election Results of 2020 OUT and declare the RIGHTFUL WINNER, or do you have a NEW ELECTION? A Massive Fraud of this type and magnitude allows for the termination of all rules, regulations, and articles, even those found in the Constitution.'[84] It has begun to looks as though, in some Western democracies, the legal system cannot even maintain the appearance of democracy: if it wants to survive, to appear democratic, it has to openly break its own laws. Appearances are likewise disintegrating in today's Russia: in 2014, Putin claimed that there was no Russian military intervention in Crimea, that the local

population rebelled against Ukrainian terror; later, he admitted that Russian soldiers had intervened there in uniforms
without any state symbols. Yevgeny Prigozhin, head of the
Wagner Group, at first denied that he had anything to do with
it; later, he simply admitted that he organized it.

True courage is thus being redefined as the courage to break
the laws if state interests demand it. We find this stance in the
properly Rightist admiration for the celebration of the heroes
who are ready to do the dirty work: it is easy to do a noble
thing for one's country, up to sacrificing one's life for it – it is
much more difficult to commit a crime for one's country. In his
speech to SS leaders in Posen on 4 October 1943, Himmler
spoke about the mass killing of the Jews as 'a glorious page in
our history, and one that has never been written and never can
be written'. He explicitly included the killing of women and
children: 'We faced the question: what should we do with the
women and children? I decided here too to find a completely
clear solution. I did not regard myself as justified in extermin-
ating the men – that is to say, to kill them or have them
killed – and to allow the avengers in the shape of children to
grow up for our sons and grandchildren. The difficult decision
had to be taken to have this people disappear from the earth.'

However, in Russia and some other states, something quite
different is happening simultaneously. Under the Stalinist
regime, appearances were saved because eating the last cannibal was explicitly legalized: the murderous purges of millions
represented a permanent eating of the last cannibal. (The paradox here is that, as in Sophocles' *Antigone*, the unwritten rule
that it is very risky to obey is morality itself.) Under Putin,
Russia has once again elevated eating cannibals into a law: on
15 December 2022, the state Duma adopted the first reading of
a bill saying that any offences that had been committed in

Donetsk, Luhansk, Zaporizhzhia and Kherson, before the four Ukrainian regions were annexed on 30 September that year, 'will not be considered a crime punishable by law' if they are deemed to have been 'in the interest of the Russian Federation'. It was not clear how it would be decided whether a crime had served Russia's interests. (The Russian armed forces have been accused of a wide range of crimes in the occupied regions of Ukraine, ranging from torture, rape and murder to looting and vandalism.) Are we aware of what is happening here? No wonder the metaphor of cannibalism is already circulating in critical analyses of the Ukrainian war.

Timothy Garton Ash, who wrote that 'Russian culture is a collateral victim of Putin's self-devouring cannibalism,' is quite justified in claiming that 'the time has come to ask whether, objectively speaking, Vladimir Putin is an agent of American imperialism. For no American has ever done half as much damage to what Putin calls the "Russian world" as the Russian leader himself has.' The same term occurs in a magnificent excoriation of the bullying Russian ambassador to Kazakhstan, Alexey Borodavkin, delivered in fluent Russian by the Kazakh journalist Arman Shuraev. 'Russophobia is all that you have achieved with your stupid actions,' he says. If Russia invades Kazakhstan as it has Ukraine, 'the entire Kazakh steppe will be strewn with the corpses of your conscripts . . . You are idiots. You are cannibals who eat themselves.'

Paradoxically, this false transparency makes the mystifications of the state power even more dangerous, dismantling our moral sensitivity. This is why we need figures like Julian Assange more than ever. Assange is our Antigone: kept for a long time in the position of a living corpse (in an isolated solitary cell, with very limited contacts with his family and lawyers, with no conviction or even official accusation, just waiting for the extradition) – why? Because, as a spy of the people, he made (a small part of) the obscene dark side of US policy visible to the public, rather than just informing on it to the secret services of a rival nation. What Assange disclosed in this way is the hidden solidarity of those in power, even (or especially) if they belong to regimes that publicly regard each other as enemies, advocating different ideologies and social systems. These fierce enemies have no problem in sharing a basic premise: the power structure (state apparatus) has to go on functioning.

We can learn a lot about how this works from the way that, in January 2022, the ending of David Fincher's classic film *Fight Club* was changed for the Chinese video release. In the 1999 original, the nameless narrator (played by Edward Norton) kills off his imagined ideal ego Tyler Durden (Brad Pitt) before watching buildings burst into flames in apparent confirmation that his plan to destroy modern civilization is being executed. The version now playing on China's largest video streamer stops before the buildings explode; the final scene is instead replaced with an English-language title card explaining that the anarchic plot was foiled by the authorities: 'The police rapidly figured out the whole plan and arrested all criminals, successfully preventing the bomb from exploding. After the trial, Tyler was sent to lunatic asylum receiving psychological treatment. He was discharged from the hospital in 2012.'

One cannot but note the neo-conservative tone of this change: it sustains unconditional solidarity with power, even if the power is in this case that of the American state. What's more, the disturbance is not treated as a political revolt but as a case of mental illness to be cured. It is an irony that the Chinese ending comes close to the ending of the novel on which the movie is based. The narrator finds redemption at the end of the film by getting rid of Tyler Durden as his ego ideal (shooting at himself so that the bullet passes through his cheek), and assuming full personal responsibility for the violent revolutionary act that was planned (blowing up banks that hold files on credit cards). There is no hint at pathology here – on the contrary, at this point, he becomes 'normal', so there is no longer any need for him to beat himself up; his destructive energy can be directed outwards, at social reality.

In the novel on which the movie is based, the narrator is placed in a mental institution, as he is in the Chinese version of the movie. However, the novel can still be read as a coming-of-age tale, the fact that he is placed into a mental institution being merely a sign that our society, which mis-recognizes maturity as madness, is in itself mad. This in no way holds for the Chinese version in which the Narrator's story is dismissed as a pathological case and social order is perceived as something normal to be upheld. What should give us pause is the weird fact that China, a country which legitimizes itself as a Socialist alternative to Western liberalism, changes the ending of a film that is highly critical of Western liberal society, disqualifying its critical stance as an expression of madness that should be cured in a mental institution.

Why is China doing this? There is only one consistent answer. In October 2019, Chinese media launched an offensive promoting the claim that demonstrations in Europe and South America (which were broadly protests against economic austerity measures) were in fact the direct result of Western tolerance of Hong Kong unrest. In a commentary published in *Beijing News*, the former Chinese diplomat Wang Zhen wrote that 'the disastrous impact of a "chaotic Hong Kong" has begun to influence the Western world,' suggesting that demonstrators 'in Chile and Spain' were taking their cues from Hong Kong. Along the same lines, an editorial in the *Global Times* held that 'there are many problems in the West and all kinds of undercurrents of dissatisfaction. Many of them will eventually manifest in the way the Hong Kong protests did.' What became clear was this: Communist China is discreetly playing on the solidarity of those *in power* all around the world, uniting them against the rebellious populace, warning the West not to underestimate the dissatisfaction in their own countries – as if, beneath all ideological and geo-political tensions, they all share the same basic interest: holding onto power.

And what does this mean for the ongoing war in Europe? Perhaps it allows us to see more clearly the reasons why the West got it so wrong. First, we thought they wouldn't invade. Then we thought the war would be over in days. Then, when Ukraine showed strong resistance, we thought Putin might lose. Then we thought Russia's economy would collapse because of sanctions, and Putin would be toppled. Now Russia is gaining ground, its economy is doing just fine, and Putin doesn't look like he's going anywhere.

Darker prospects lie ahead. In June 2022, meeting at their first in-person convention since 2018, Texan Republicans passed motions declaring that President Joe Biden 'was not legitimately elected' and rebuking Senator John Cornyn for taking part in bipartisan gun talks. They also approved a position that declared homosexuality 'an abnormal lifestyle choice' and called for Texan schoolchildren 'to learn about the humanity of the preborn child'. The first measure, declaring that President Joe Biden 'was not legitimately elected', was a clear step in the direction of the (for the time being 'cold') civil war in the US: it delegitimizes the existing political order. If we combine this and other signs that the Republican Party is more than ever controlled by Trump with the Ukraine war fatigue, a worrying possibility opens up: what if Trump or DeSantis win the next Presidential election and enforce a pact with Russia, abandoning Ukrainians in the same way Trump did with the Kurds in Syria?

During the Maidan uprising in 2013, a telephone call made by the US diplomat Victoria Nuland was leaked. During the call, she casually stated 'Fuck the EU!' – a clear signal that the US was pursuing its own goals in Ukraine. Putin has also for years consistently pursued the politics of 'Fuck Europe!', of dismantling it through support for Brexit, Catalonian separatism, le Pen in France, Salvini in Italy . . . This anti-European axis that unites Putin with certain trends in US politics is one of the most dangerous elements in today's situation, and it confronts the African, Asian, and Latino-American countries with a difficult dilemma. If they follow the old anti-European instinct and lean towards Russia, what awaits us is a sad new world.

The Russian version of events (adopted even by some Western Leftists) holds that the Maidan uprising – the wave of demonstrations and civil unrest in Ukraine, which began on 21 November 2013 with large protests in Maidan Nezalezhnosti (Independence Square) in Kyiv – was a Nazi putsch against a democratically elected government, carefully orchestrated by the US. Of course the events were chaotic, with many different tendencies and foreign interferences, but, whatever it was, Maidan was at its most basic an authentic popular revolt. During the uprising, Maidan was turned into a huge protest camp occupied by thousands of protesters and protected by makeshift barricades. It had kitchens, first aid posts and broadcasting facilities, as well as stages for speeches, lectures, debates and performances – in other words, it was as far from a Nazi putsch as you could imagine. It was, rather, much closer to what went on in Hong Kong, in Istanbul, or during the Arab Spring.

The Maidan uprising can and should also be compared with the

Belarus protests of 2020–21, which were brutally quashed. But in no way should the 6 January 2021 attack on the Capitol be called the US Maidan. Some of my friends were totally traumatized by the scenes of the mob invading the Capitol: 'The crowd taking over the seat of power – we should be doing that! The wrong people are doing it!' This, maybe, is why the populist Right annoys the Left so much: the Rightists are stealing all the Left's fun.

Recall what Putin said on 21 February 2022: after claiming that Ukraine was a Bolshevik creation, he went on to allege that

> today the 'grateful progeny' [of Lenin] has toppled monuments to Lenin in Ukraine. They call it decommunization. You want decommunization? Very well, this suits us just fine. But why stop halfway? We are ready to show what real decommunization would mean for Ukraine.'[85]

Putin's logic is clear: Ukraine was a Bolshevik (Lenin's) creation, so true decommunization means the end of Ukraine. But do not forget also that 'decommunization' should be taken here literally: an effort to erase the last traces of the welfare-state legacy.

This brings us back to our main concern. For years, Russia and China have been gripped with panic whenever a popular rebellion explodes somewhere in their domain of influence, and as a rule they interpret it as a plot instigated by the West, as the work of foreign propagandists and agents. China is now at least honest enough to admit that there is a deep dissatisfaction everywhere around the world. The problem is just that its response does not acknowledge the cause of popular discontent; instead, it appeals to the solidarity of those in power, whichever side of the new ideological divide they are on. But what if we remain faithful to the Leftist tradition and maintain the solidarity of those who rebel?

Lenin in Ukraine Today

There are situations in which a principled decision is not enough, and a well-thought-through strategic choice between bad and worse is needed. Bolivia has perhaps the world's largest reserves of lithium and now plans to begin to extract them, but ecologists are strictly opposed to this, since extraction is highly polluting, even if it is done to high environmental standards. However, why should poor Bolivia sacrifice itself and refuse to become the Saudi Arabia of lithium when developed Western economies are continuing to pollute the environment to a much greater degree?

And the same holds for Ukraine – it is not enough just to call for negotiations and offer moral support. So what should we do, how far should we go toward helping Ukraine without risking a new world war? Should arms be sent to Ukraine (as is already going on)? Should a no-fly zone be declared? Lenin thought a big war might create conditions for a revolution – but now we need some kind of revolution to prevent a war. Remember what the Russian Foreign Minister Sergei Lavrov said in February 2022: if a Third World War were to take place, it would involve nuclear weapons. We know that years ago Putin publicly stated that, if, in a future war, Russia were to lose the ground battle, if would be ready to use nuclear weapons first. As we've already established, Mao Zedong was wrong: when paper tigers are doing badly in a war, they are even more dangerous than real ones.

One should not be too much of a pessimist – even if Russia somehow occupies all of Ukraine, Ukraine is already preparing for partisan warfare, distributing huge numbers of guns to ordinary men and women. But we should also have no illusions: the war between Russia and NATO has already begun, although it has been till now mostly fought through proxies. Russia is already intervening in Bosnia and Kosovo, and, as Lavrov mentioned, Russia's final ambition is to demilitarize all of Europe. So, again, we need not just principled decisions but well-calculated, strategic thinking and actions.

The key to unifying a fanatical principled stance and ruthless pragmatism is the ability to analyse a concrete situation in such a way that we distil it into a single, abstract choice, neglecting the myriad inessential features that surround it. A maths problem went viral towards the end of 2022 when it became known that Chinese 5th graders (ten or eleven years old) were asked the question: 'If a ship has twenty-six sheep and ten goats on board, how old is the ship's captain?' The Chinese authorities explained that the question was used in exams in order to instigate critical thinking. Obviously, the correct answer is, 'There is not enough data available to provide an answer.' Some individuals, however, provided an ingenious if rough reply based on their knowledge of Chinese law: to be a captain of a boat carrying more than 5 tons of cargo (twenty-six sheep and ten goats weigh around 7 tons), one has to work as a captain of a smaller boat for at least five years; and the youngest one can become the captain of a boat is twenty-three years; so, the captain should be at least twenty-eight years old. It was soon realized that, for the same reason, a similar question had been put to pupils in France, and later to pupils in some other neighbouring countries. The surprise was just how many students produced an answer by way of desperately trying to read some meaning into the numbers; unfortunately the most common reply was that, since 26 + 10 = 36, this must be the captain's age . . . The lesson is this: we must not succumb to the temptation of reading meaning into numbers, especially in an age obsessed with statistics. At a more general level, it is essential to remember that, when solving a precise problem, one has to learn to ignore irrelevant data.[86] Thinking does not involve taking into account the infinite complexity of every situation – on the contrary, thinking begins by learning to abstract, to ignore the extraneous detail. This holds from ideology to quantum physics – is not one of our preferred ideological procedures to explain a phenomenon like unexpected economic success through the personal features of the individual who got rich ('he worked really hard, he is really bright')? When we read about an instantaneous (i.e. faster than light) link between particles, most of us as a rule continue to refer to our ordinary notion of space and time, and then try to imagine the almost-infinite speed of the information that connects the particles in question. And this holds especially for radical emancipatory politics – at its core is the art of combining fidelity to the Cause with the most ruthless pragmatic and strategic adjustments in pursuing this Cause. The unsurpassable model is here still Lenin, as Adam Tooze explains:

On 14 May [1918] Lenin proposed that the German imperialism should be offered a comprehensive plan of economic cooperation. By way of justification he offered what was surely the weirdest of his many modifications of orthodox Marxism. The need for a close alliance between the Russian revolution and the Imperial Germany, he argued, arose out of the twisted logic of history itself. History had by 1918 'taken such a *peculiar course* that it has given birth . . . to two unconnected halves of socialism existing side by side, like two future chickens in the single shell of international imperialism.

[For Lenin,] Germany's legendary wartime economic organization [. . .] was 'the most striking embodiment of the material realization of the economic, the productive and the socio-economic conditions for socialism'.[87]

One should notice here than Lenin does not speak about the development of German productive forces but about 'economic organization', about the concrete way relations between people are organized in big industrial companies in a wartime economy. What this means is that socialism should take over this organization, putting it under the control of the state. How serious Lenin was about this idea of cooperation with Germany is demonstrated by another detail: after the British established an anti-Bolshevik front at Murmansk, the Bolshevik government officially asked Germany to intervene with military force to stabilize it, that is, to keep the British army from advancing south. Even Rosa Luxemburg was shocked at this idea, but nothing came from it because of German wavering.[88] The lesson of such paradoxes is very clear: what characterizes authentic emancipatory thought is not a vision of a conflict-free harmonious future, but the properly dialectical notion of *antagonism*, which is totally incompatible with the (insatiable) Rightist need for an enemy against which to assert our self-identity.

What does such a stance (to which I fully submit) imply for Ukraine today? One thing is sure: till the 2022 war, the large majority in Ukraine was bilingual, jumping from Russian to Ukrainian and back without any great worry. The Russian invasion achieved not only the unification of Western Europe; it also gave a big boost precisely to what Russia denies the existence of: a distinct Ukrainian identity as opposed to, even exclusive of, Russian identity. The repressed 'Ukrainization' of the 1920s is returning exactly 100 years later – but this time it sounds a very different political note. There can be no excuse for some of the decisions Ukraine – and some of the Baltic states – have taken in recent years, such as rehabilitating certain Nazi collaborators (who were actively involved in the mass liquidations of Jews and Russian prisoners) as first heroes of the anti-Communist resistance. In 2019 the Ukrainian parliament declared 1 January a National Day of Commemoration for Stepan Bandera, who briefly joined forces with the Nazi occupation of Ukraine; some of his supporters at the Organization of Ukrainian Nationalists, which he headed, committed countless war crimes against Jews. Despite all this, Bandera was elevated to the status of Hero of Ukraine by the ex-president Viktor Yushchenko, and statues of him now abound in Ukraine. The region of Lviv, Bandera's native city, declared 2019 'Stepan Bandera Year,' sparking protests by Israel. Ukraine's State Committee on Television and Radio Broadcasting banned *The Book of Thieves* by the Swedish historian Anders Rydell: the decree cited the book's 'inciting ethnic, racial and religious hatred', which meant Rydell's critical analysis of the actions of Symon Petliura, another nationalist whose troops murdered countless Jews in pogroms.[89] Not to mention the fact that radical nationalists in Ukraine have proposed the prohibition of the use of Russian language in public space. This is the reason why Israel maintains its neutrality in the ongoing war and is not ready to condemn Russia. If Ukraine seriously means to find a path to emancipation, to join 'civilized' nations, the first step must be to bring out and clearly condemn all participation in the Holocaust, the 'non-civilized' act par excellence.

To avoid a fatal misunderstanding, this does not imply any kind of relativization of the Russian invasion in the vulgar sense that 'nobody's hands are clean' – Russia committed an unthinkably horrible act. This is the truth of the situation – however, in his perspicuous analysis of the imbroglios of modern European revolutions that culminated in Stalinism, Jean-Claude Milner insists on the radical gap that separates exactitude (factual truth, accuracy about facts) and Truth (the Cause to which we are committed):

> When one admits the radical difference between exactitude and truth, only one ethical maxim remains: never oppose the two. Never make of the inexact the privileged means of the effects of truth. Never transform these effects into by-products of the lie. Never make the real into an instrument of the conquest of reality.'[90]

Applied to Ukraine, this means: we should never allow the basic truth of the situation and the choice imposed by it (to support Ukraine) to obfuscate facts in all their confusion and ambiguity (as in: 'now is not the right moment to bring out the dark sides of Ukraine'). Russia's justifications for its invasion are lies, but they are sometimes lies in the guise of partial small truths, which should be openly dealt with. It is in the interest of Ukrainians themselves, of advancing their Cause, that we bring out all their mistakes and small lies (like the occasional denial of the greatness of Russian culture). If we deny or ignore them, we act as if their Cause can only be sustained by such lies. Ukrainians don't deserve this: there are many small sublime acts which attest to the greatness of their Cause.

What Will Grow Out of a Pocket Full of Sunflower Seeds?

Back in the first week of Russia's invasion of Ukraine, Michel Marder published a wonderful essay in *Salon* magazine – wonderful because it did what is most needed today: it added a deeper philosophical dimension to our reactions to the Ukrainian catastrophe.[91] It describes an incident which brought to my mind Agatha Christie's Miss Marple novel *A Pocket Full of Rye,* in which a rich London businessman dies after drinking his morning tea, and a search of his clothing reveals a quantity of rye in his jacket pocket. In the novel, the reason rye is found there is that a 'pocket full of rye' is part of a nursery rhyme referred to by the murderer.

This brings us to Ukraine, where something uncannily similar happened – only not with rye but with sunflower seeds. Marder describes how, in Henichesk, a port city on the sea of Azov, an old Ukrainian woman confronted a heavily armed Russian soldier and offered him sunflower seeds to put in his pocket – so that they might bloom when he died and his body rotting in the earth might be of some value, feeding the growing plant.[92]

What disturbed me about this gesture was the lack of sympathy for ordinary Russian soldiers, many of whom were sent on a mission to Ukraine without proper food supplies and other provisions, some not even knowing where they were, or why; there have even been reports of Ukrainians bringing them food. It brought back my memories from Prague, 1968: I arrived there one day before the Soviet invasion, and was left wandering around the city for a couple of days till transport for foreigners was organized. What immediately struck me was the confusion and poverty of ordinary soldiers, in clear contrast to the officers, of whom the soldiers were much more afraid than us, the protesting demonstrators.

Even in these crazy times, we should not be ashamed of sticking to the last vestiges of normality and invoking popular culture. So let me mention another Christie classic, *The Hollow*, in which the eccentric Lucy Angkatell has invited the Christows (John, a top Harley street doctor, and his wife Gerda), along with other members of her extended family, to her estate for the weekend. Hercule Poirot (who is staying nearby in his country cottage) is also invited to dinner; the next morning he witnesses a scene that seems strangely staged: Gerda Christow stands with a gun in her hand next to John's body, as it bleeds into the swimming pool. Lucy, Henrietta (John's lover) and Edward (a cousin of Lucy's and a second cousin of Henrietta) are also present. John utters a final urgent appeal, 'Henrietta!', and dies. It seems obvious that Gerda is the murderer.

Henrietta steps forward to take the revolver from her hand, but apparently fumbles and drops it into the swimming pool, destroying the evidence. Poirot realizes that the dying man's 'Henrietta' was a call to his lover to protect his wife from imprisonment for his own death – without a conscious plan, the entire family has joined the plot and deliberately misdirected Poirot, as they each know Gerda is the murderer, and are attempting to save her.

This is a smart reversal of the standard formula, whereby a murder is committed, there is a group of suspects who have the motive and opportunity to do it and, even if the culprit seems obvious, the detective uncovers clues which belie the murder scene staged by the true murderer to cover his tracks. Instead, Christie's group of suspects generate clues implicating themselves to cover up the fact that the true murderer *is* the obvious one who was caught at the scene of the crime with a gun in her hand. So the murder scene is staged, but in a reflexive way: the deception resides in the very fact that it appears to be artificial, to be staged – the truth masks itself as artifice, so that the true fakes are 'clues' themselves – or, as Jane Marple says in yet another Christie classic, *They Do It with Mirrors*: 'Never underestimate the power of the obvious.'

This should remind us of the way ideology functions, today especially: it presents itself as something mysterious, pointing towards a hidden backdrop, to cover up the crime that it is committing (or legitimizing) openly. Which is why, at some level, one should ignore the hidden 'complexity' of the situation and trust what is right before our eyes.

So what is effectively going on? Remember the time before the pandemic, when the climate crisis was in the headlines? It was eclipsed by the arrival of Covid, which became the big news in our media. But once the Russian invasion of Ukraine began, the pandemic all but disappeared; it was Ukraine in the headlines. And if anything, the fear we feel today is now much greater, much more acute: there is almost a nostalgia for the good old two years of fighting the pandemic, or for the time before that, when the only danger on the scene was some apparently distant threat of warming. This sudden shift demonstrates the limit of our freedom – nobody chose this change, it just happened (except for conspiracy theorists who claim that the Ukrainian crisis is another plot by the establishment to continue with the emergency state and keep us under control).

Despite the fact of very real ongoing threats posed by viruses and heatwaves, droughts, famines and floods, we are now, in

2023, captivated by the war. Even some Leftists are hoodwinked, and see Putin and Aleksandr Dugin as opponents of the global capitalist order, as advocates of irreducible diversity of ethnic-cultural identities. But the diversity advocated by Dugin is a diversity based on ethnic identities, not diversity within ethnic groups – which is why 'only war could decide really'. The rise of fundamentalist ethnic identities is ultimately the other side of the global capitalist coin, not its opposite. We urgently need more globalization, not less: we need global solidarity and cooperation more than ever if we seriously want to cope with the immediate threats we face, foremost among them global warming.

G. K. Chesterton wrote: 'Take away the supernatural and what you are left with is the unnatural.' We should endorse this statement, but in the opposite sense, not in the sense intended by Chesterton: we should accept that nature is 'un-natural', a freak show of contingent disturbances with no inner rhyme or reason. At the end of June 2021, a 'heat dome' – a weather phenomenon where a ridge of high pressure traps and compresses warm air, driving up temperatures and baking a region – over the north-west of the US and the south-west of Canada caused temperatures to approach 50 degrees Celsius, so that Vancouver was hotter than the Middle East. True, a 'heat dome' is a local phenomenon, but it is the result of a global disturbance that clearly depends on human interventions in the natural cycles, so we have to act against it globally.

This, of course, in no way implies that we should treat the Ukrainian war as a relatively unimportant local conflict – we should just always maintain a global perspective and locate the ongoing war in the series of other crises, and understand what it implies for the gradual disintegration of global capitalism. So what can we do? And what can we learn from Putin? Remember how, a day or two after the outbreak of the war,

Putin called for the Ukrainian army to overthrow Zelensky's government and take over, claiming that it would be much easier to negotiate peace with them. Maybe, it would be good for something like this to happen in Russia itself (where, in 1953, Marshall Zhukov did help Khruschev to overthrow Beria). So, does this mean we should simply demonize Putin? No – as we've seen, to really counter Putin, we have to gather the courage to take a critical look at ourselves.

What games has the liberal West been playing with Russia over the last three decades? Didn't it effectively push Russia towards Fascism – just remember the catastrophic economic 'advice' given to Russia in the Yeltsin years? Yes, Putin was obviously preparing for this war for some time, but the West knew it, so the war is absolutely not an unexpected shock. In fact, there are good reasons to believe that the West was consciously pushing Russia into a corner. Though it does nothing to justify their attack on Ukraine, the Russian fear of being encircled by NATO is far from being the figment of a paranoiac imagination. There is a moment of truth in what none other than Viktor Orbán said:

> How did the war come about? We're caught in the crossfire between major geopolitical players: NATO has been expanding eastwards, and Russia has become less and less comfortable with that. The Russians made two demands: that Ukraine declare its neutrality, and that NATO would not admit Ukraine. These security guarantees weren't given to the Russians, so they decided to take them by force of arms. This is the geopolitical significance of this war.[93]

This small truth, of course, covers up a Big Lie: the crazy geopolitical game Russia is pursuing – but we should never ignore such details or dismiss them as unimportant, in the same way that we should never succumb to the temptation of ignoring small lies on behalf of a Big Truth. This is why, as for the situation now, there should be no taboos preventing critical analysis. Obviously, as we have already seen, the Ukrainian side also cannot be unconditionally trusted, and the situation in the Donbas region is far from clear. Furthermore, the wave of exclusions of Russian artists is approaching madness. When the war broke out, the Bicocca university in Milan, Italy, suspended a series of lectures on Dostoyevsky's novels by Paolo Nori with an argument that is very Putinian: it is just a preventive gesture to keep the situation calm . . .[94] (The suspension was cancelled a couple of days later.) But cultural contact with Russia is now more important than ever. And what about the mega-scandal of only allowing Ukrainians to enter Europe, and not the Third World students and workers in Ukraine who are also trying to escape the war?

The horror of our correspondents and commentators at what is going on in Ukraine is understandable but profoundly ambiguous. It can mean: now that we have seen that such horrors are not limited to the Third World, that they are not just something we watch comfortably on our screens, that they can also happen here, we understand that if we want to live safely we should fight them everywhere. But it can also mean: let the horrors remain there, far away, let's just protect ourselves from them. Yes, they are correct, Putin is a war criminal – but did we only discover this now? Was he not already a war criminal a couple of years ago when, in order to save the Assad regime, Russian planes were bombing Aleppo, the largest city in Syria, and in a much more brutal way than they are doing now in Kyiv? We knew it then, but our indignation was purely moral and verbal. The feeling of a much greater sympathy for

Ukrainians who are 'like us' shows the limit of Frederic Lordon's attempt to ground emancipatory politics in the sense of 'belonging' sustained by what Spinoza called transindividual 'imitation of affects' – we have to develop solidarity for those with whom we do not share affective belonging.

Ukraine was the poorest country of all the post-Soviet states. Even if Ukrainians – hopefully – win, their victorious defence will be their moment of truth. They will have to learn the lesson that it is not enough for them to 'catch up' with the West, since Western liberal democracy is itself in a deep crisis. If a Europe that excludes the 'uncivilized' triumphs, then we don't need Russia to destroy us – we will successfully accomplish the task on our own.

The Unmistakable Signs of Ethical Decay

One of the most reliable measures of ethical progress is the rise of a certain kind of dogmatism. In a normal country there is no debate over if or when rape and torture are tolerable: the public 'dogmatically' accepts that they are out of the question, and those who advocate such things are simply dismissed as freaks. A clear sign of ethical decay is that we begin to debate rape (are there 'legitimate rapes'?), or that torture is not only silently tolerated but publicly displayed. Gradually, things become possible which were previously unimaginable. Here is the latest case: in November 2022, Yevgeny Prigozhin responded to an unverified video distributed on Telegram. The video shows a man identified as Yevgeny Nuzhin, a former Russian prisoner who had been conscripted as a Wagner Group mercenary, being executed after admitting that he had changed sides in September to 'fight against the Russians'. Nuzhin explains that he was abducted in Kyiv on 11 October, and came round in a cellar. As he says these words, an unidentified man loitering in combat clothing behind him smashes a sledgehammer into the side of his head and neck. The video was posted under the title 'The Hammer of Revenge'. Asked to comment on the execution video, Prigozhin said in remarks released by his spokeswoman that the video should be called 'A Dog Receives a Dog's Death'.[95]

But this is not the whole story: at the end of November 2022, Prigozhin's Wagner Group sent a 'bloodied' sledge-hammer in a violin case to the European Parliament after members started proceedings to label them as terrorists. It released a video depicting a suited lawyer working for Wagner Group carrying a violin case into a bare room and placing it on a table; he lifts the lid of the violin case, showing off a highly polished sledgehammer, its head engraved with Wagner's logo and the handle daubed with red paint to depict blood. Prigozhin commented that he was sending the sledgehammer to the European Parliament as 'information' before its members took their decision.[96] And the story goes on: Al Jazeera later reported that

> A Ukrainian official said that Ukrainian embassies and consulates in six European countries have recently received packages containing animals' eyes. Ministry of Foreign Affairs spokesman Oleh Nikolenko wrote on Facebook that the 'bloody parcels' were received by the Ukrainian embassies in Hungary, the Netherlands, Poland, Croatia and Italy, and by consulates in Naples, Italy; Krakow, Poland and the Czech city of Brno.[97]

No wonder these events were commented upon by the media as proof that 'Putin's Private Army Goes Full ISIS'[98], referring to the way that ISIS publicly executes its prisoners (making them confess and then cutting their throats by a knife, before releasing video recordings of the ordeal on the web). And no wonder that Iran is now a close ally of Russia: both countries are moving in the same direction. Among those arrested and executed for participating in the recent wave of Iranian protests are hundreds of young girls. Iran is one of the world's last countries to execute 'juvenile offenders', and the age of criminal responsibility is just nine for girls, while it is fifteen for boys. Iranian law prohibits the execution of a minor if they're a virgin – a roadblock which, according to reports in

Australia, 'has been solved in the past by marrying the girls off to prison guards to be raped the night before their murders – a practice that's been documented over the decades by journalists, families, activists and even a former leader'.[99]

Now things are getting really twisted: Israel (which proudly presents itself as a democratic country) is getting closer and closer to being a fundamentalist-religious country, not unlike its Arab fundamentalist neighbours. Take the fact that Itamar Ben-Gvir is now serving in Netanyahu's government as the Minister for National Security. Before entering politics, Ben-Gvir was known to have a portrait in his living room of Israeli-American terrorist Baruch Goldstein, who in 1994 massacred twenty-nine Palestinian Muslim worshippers and wounded 125 others in Hebron, in what became known as the Cave of the Patriarchs massacre. He entered politics by joining the youth movement of the Kach and Kahane Chai party, which was designated as a terrorist organization and outlawed by the Israeli government. When he came of age for conscription into the Israel Defense Forces at 18, he was barred from service due to his extreme-right political background. In the 2022 Israeli legislative election, Ben-Gvir's party had an unprecedented success, more than doubling its votes from the 2021 election, becoming the third largest party in the 25th Knesset.[100] Another signal of the same decay: during an interview with *The Blaze*, Netanyahu recently said that

> antisemitism has taken on a pernicious new form, because it's not fashionable to say you're an anti-Semite. You say, 'Well, I'm anti-Zionist' – You don't even say, 'I'm anti-Israel,' you say, 'I'm anti-Zionist. Well, I'm not against the Jews, I just don't think they should have a state of their own.' It's like, 'I'm not anti-American, I just don't think you should be an American.'[101]

Wouldn't a much more appropriate comparison be: 'It's like, "I'm not anti-Palestinian, I just don't think they should have a state of their own"'? This brings us to the key question: is criticizing Israeli occupation of the West Bank denying Israel's right to exist? Things get here much darker: Netanyahu recently called for a fight against rising Muslim and left-wing anti-Semitism in Europe, hours after a report on anti-Semitism released by the Diaspora Affairs Ministry documented a worldwide increase in attacks against Jews last year.[102] Why does Netanyahu ignore far-right anti-Semitism? Because he relies on it: the new Right in the West are anti-Semitic in their own country, but staunchly support the existence of the state of Israel as a barrier against Muslim invasion. Zionist anti-Semitism is a sobering fact.

Similar cases abound. Take Jarosław Kaczyński, the leader of Poland's ruling Law and Justice party, who recently claimed that Poland's low birth rate is mainly caused by young women drinking too much alcohol[103] – so it's not socio-economic conditions but simply women's drinking. Even if Kaczyński's suggestion were to contain a grain of truth – which, I think, it doesn't – we should still explain what social pressures push young women to search for solace in drinking. To respond by placing the blame with 'LGBT+ ideology' is clearly ridiculous.

When 'decent' liberal democracy still predominated, radical Leftists liked to point out that this was only a mask concealing the obscene violent truth. Now I am tempted to say: 'Please bring back the mask!'

Unfortunately, all this is just one side of the story. We have today two main opposed ideological blocs. The religious neo-conservatives (from Putin and Trump to Iran) advocate a return to old orthodox Christian (or Muslim) traditions against 'Satanic' postmodern decadence – usually focussing on LGBT+ and transgender issues; however, their actual politics is full of barbarian obscenity and violence. On the opposite side, the Politically Correct liberal Left preaches permissiveness to all forms of sexual and ethnic identity; however, in its endeavour to guarantee this tolerance, it needs more and more rules – more 'cancelling' and regulating – which introduce constant anxiety and tension in this ostensibly happy permissive universe. These limitations are in some sense much stronger than the paternal prohibition that solicits the desire for transgression, and they do little to help the cause of genuine emancipation – they distract from it. One cannot understand the messy reaction of the 'democratic' West to the Ukrainian war without this ideological struggle in the West which sometimes comes close to a civil war.

Duane Rouselle's characterization of woke as 'racism in the time of the many without the One' may appear problematic, but it hits the mark: in almost exact opposition to the typical posture of the racist – who fights against a foreign intruder posing a threat to the unity of the One (say, immigrants and Jews to our Nation) – the 'woke' position reacts against those who are suspected not to have truly abandoned their attachment to old forms of the One (in other words, 'patriots', proponents of patriarchal values, Eurocentrists . . .).

In this 'new world order', all sexual orientations are acceptable with one exception: white cisgender men, who are enjoined to feel guilty just for what they are, for being 'comfortable in their skin', while all others (even cis women) are allowed to be what they (feel that they) are. This stance is more and more discernible in weird occurrences all around us. Let's take the case of Gettysburg College, which, amid understandable widespread backlash, postponed an event in 2022 for people who are 'tired of white cis men'. The event was due to have been hosted by the Gender and Sexuality Resource

Center, and 'attendees were encouraged to "come paint & write about" their frustrations with white "comfortable in skin" men.'[104] As expected, many accused the college of harbouring racism. White cis men themselves were probably also expected to participate in the event, although in a self-critical way, expressing their discomfort with regard to their skin and their guilt with regard to their sexual orientation.

It is in these terms that we can account for the paradox of how, in woke and cancel culture, non-binary fluidity coincides with its opposite. The prestigious École normale supérieure in Paris has debated a proposal to establish in their dormitories corridors reserved exclusively for individuals who have chosen mixity/diversity (*mixité choisie*) as their gender identity, with the exclusion of cisgender men (men whose sense of personal identity and gender corresponds with their birth sex).[105] The proposed rules are strict – for example, those who do not fit the criteria would not be allowed to pass even briefly through these corridors. The idea also opens up the path to further boundaries: if enough individuals identify in more specific terms, they can be reserved a corridor. One should note three features of this proposal: first, that it excludes only cisgender men, not cisgender women; second, it is not based on any objective criteria of classification but only on subjective self-designation; third, it calls for further classificatory subdivisions, demonstrating how all the emphasis on plasticity, choice and diversity ends up in what one cannot but call a new apartheid, a new network of fixed identities. This is why the woke stance provides the supreme case of how permissiveness turns over into universal prohibition: in a politically correct regime, we never know if and when some of us will be cancelled for our acts or words: the criteria are always murky.

With all its declared opposition to the new forms of

barbarism, the woke Left fully participates in it, promoting and practising a flat discourse without irony. Although it advocates pluralism and promotes difference, its subjective position of enunciation – the place from which it speaks – is extremely authoritarian, allowing very limited debate and imposing exclusions that are often based on arbitrary premises. However, in all this mess, we should always bear in mind that wokeism and cancel culture are *de facto* limited to the narrow world of academia (and, up to a point, some intellectual professions like journalism), while society at large moves in the opposite direction. Cancel culture with its implicit paranoia is a desperate (and obviously inefficient) attempt to compensate for the actual troubles and tragedies faced by LGBT+ individuals, the violence and exclusion to which they are permanently subjected. The answer to this violence cannot be a retreat into a cultural fortress, a pseudo 'safe space' whose discursive fanaticism leaves intact and even strengthens the resistance of the majority to it.

Contrary to those who say that wokeism is receding from academic and cultural life, I think that it is, rather, being gradually 'normalized', widely accepted even by those who privately doubt its tenets, and practised by the majority of educational and state institutions. This is why more than ever it deserves our criticism – together with its opposite, the obscenity of new populism and religious fundamentalism.

At its worst, cancel culture has a distinctly fundamentalist tone – a particular thing that you said or did can be unexpectedly elevated into the universal status of an unforgivable mistake. This means that a particular case (an expression you used, for example) is condemned not because it doesn't fit same clear universal rule; rather, a new spin is given to the universality itself. No wonder, then, that obscene Rightist populists like to provoke PC activists – that they enjoy their status of the privileged object of what Lacan called *hainamoration*, an object others love to hate. I have noticed the same stance when talking to my Serb acquaintances: many of them like to complain that everybody hates them, perceiving them as 'ethnic cleansers' responsible for the atrocious crime in Srebrenica. But is this really the case? I think this feeling of being treated as a pariah is a defensive move: the reality is that now, with all the other troubles we are in, people around the globe are more and more indifferent towards Serbia (and towards Right populists in general); they don't care about the Serbs, so what is beneath Serbs' complaint is rather a desperate desire to remain a centre of attention, even as an object of hatred – better hatred than indifference. In other words, what Serbs really miss is that they are no longer the fascinating object of *hainamoration*.

Against False Awakenings

What is really sad is that we find in wokeness numerous traces of the covering up of the immanent antagonisms of social life – and it is this, as expected, that generates the need for an enemy. Think of today's arguments around the use of the pronoun 'they', which concerns much more than changes in the everyday use of language: it imply a new vision of the universality of human beings. In February 2023, the University of Kent offered guidance on pronouns to its students and staff: everyone should be called 'they' until you know their pronouns. The institution says these are guidelines, not policies, and are there as a useful resource and support tool which will help them create 'an authentic culture of inclusion' at the institution.[106] The first adequate counter-argument to such reasoning, offered by a commenter on an online forum, is this:

> There isn't anything wrong with including 'they/them' pronouns as an option. However, there is something definitely wrong with making that the ONLY [primary] option. Simply including 'they/them' as an option would be fine but actually EXCLUDING traditional pronouns [as a primary option] is not. Most trans people prefer 'she/her' or 'he/him', so making everyone 'they/them', while it is nice for non-binary people, isn't inclusive for most trans OR cisgender people. Most trans women will use female pronouns (she/her) and most trans men will use male pronouns (he/him).[107]

So we get an 'authentic culture of inclusion' which renders the pronouns used by a large majority of people secondary, subordinate. The implications of the proposed change are much more radical than it may appear: 'they' as gender-neutral is now not just an option but a neutral universal ground for all humans, so we are no longer dealing just with pluralizing positions but with the imposition of a new universality: we are all 'they', and some can additionally choose 'he' or 'she'. So why not simply endorse this solution? What gets lost in it is sexual difference itself – not as a binary order but as an antagonism that cuts across humanity. There are no 'humans' as such, this universality is constitutively traversed by an antagonism, a failure, and with 'they' as the baseline, we get again a flat universalism . . . and, as expected, this flat universalism also needs an enemy: those who don't agree with it also quickly proclaimed homophobic, reactionary, or whatever.

The consequences of such a reductive stance are more and more palpable. Take this recent example from Scotland. In December 2022, the Sturgeon government hailed a 'historic day for equality' after MSPs approved plans to make it easier and less intrusive for individuals to legally change their gender, extending the new system of self-identification to 16- and 17-year-olds. An (expected) problem emerged when a trans woman, Isla Bryson, was remanded to a women's prison in Stirling after being convicted of rapes that she had committed before she transitioned. Bryson came out as transgender only after appearing in court on a rape charge. The problem here is clear: if maleness and femaleness has nothing to do with one's body, and everything to do with one's self-definition, then one must put a trans woman convicted of rape in prison with cis women. After a wave of protests, Bryson was put into a male prison – but again, this is problematic since we have now a woman in a male prison.[108] The point here is that there is no easy solution, because sexual identity is in itself not a simple form of identity but a complex notion full of inconsistencies, tensions and unconscious features – and these are not just facts of inner psychic life; they are embedded in antagonisms which traverse the entire social body. In our official ideological space, wokeness and conservative religious fundamentalism appear as incompatible opposites – but are they really? Almost a decade ago, a Kurdish ex-Muslim, Maryam Namazie, was invited by London's Goldsmiths College to give a talk on the topic 'Apostasy, Blasphemy and Free Expression in the Age of ISIS'; her talk – which focused on the oppression of women – was repeatedly disrupted by Muslim students, as well as, ironically, the college Feminist Society, which formally aligned itself with ISOC, Goldsmith's Islamic Society.[109]

Today, the Ukrainian war offers another breathtaking example of a similarly surprising alliance: when Sahra Wagenknecht, the most popular representative of die Linke, the German Leftist party, organized and spoke at a meeting for peace in Dresden in February 2023, calling for the end of sending arms to Ukraine, Björn Höcke (one of the leading members of the extreme Right Alternative for Germany present at the meeting) shouted at her: *'Ich bitte Sie, kommen Sie zu uns!'* ('Please come to us!'), calling on her to change her party affiliation – and the public applauded him.[110] The extreme Right inviting extreme Left to join forces on behalf of German national sovereignty . . .

In the case of Namazie, the unexpected solidarity between the feminist and Islamic societies is a forceful reminder of the similarity in form of the two discourses: wokeness *de facto* works as a secularized religious dogma, with all the contradictions this implies. John McWhorter has enumerated some of them: 'You must strive eternally to understand the experiences of black people' but 'You can never understand what it is to be black, and if you think you do, you're a racist'; 'Show interest in multiculturalism' but 'Do not culturally appropriate. What is not your culture is not for you, and you may not try it or do it.'[111] This may seem like an exaggeration, but Vincent Lloyd's report on his encounter with wokeness at its worst shows that it is not. Lloyd's essay should be obligatory reading for everyone who doubts the repressive potential of wokeness, and is worth quoting *in extenso*. His credentials are impeccable: a black professor and director of the Center for Political Theology at Villanova University, he directs his university's black-studies programme, leads anti-racism and transformative-justice workshops, and publishes books on anti-black racism and prison abolition (like his classic *Black Dignity: The Struggle against Domination*).

In the Summer of 2022, Lloyd was asked by the Telluride Association to lead a six-week seminar on 'Race and the Limits of Law in America' attended by twelve carefully selected 17-year-olds. Four weeks later, the number of attendants was reduced by two (the previous week, students had voted two classmates out of the house), and he was next to be suspended from the seminar by a vote. In his last class,

> each student read from a prepared statement about how the seminar perpetuated anti-black violence in its content and form, how the black students had been harmed, how I was guilty of countless micro-aggressions, including through my body language, and how students didn't feel safe because I didn't immediately correct views that failed to treat anti-blackness as the cause of all the world's ills.[112]

Lloyd locates the origin of the trend that culminated in this event in 'that moment in the 1970s when leftist organizations imploded, the need to match and raise the militancy of one's comrades leading to a toxic culture filled with dogmatism and disillusion'. His critics relied on a series of dogmas, among them: 'There is no hierarchy of oppressions – except for anti-black oppression, which is in a class of its own. Trust black women. Prison is never the answer. All non-black people, and many black people, are guilty of anti-blackness.'

But more crucial than content was the conflict of forms between seminar and workshop. Lloyd tried to practise the seminar, an exchange of opinions: one intervention builds on another, as one student notices what another student has overlooked, and the professor guides the discussion toward the most important questions. Seminars usually focus on a classic or public text, and the participants try to patiently uncover its meaning. However, as Lloyd remarks, 'if the seminar is slow food, the anti-racist workshop put on by college-age students is a sugar rush. All the hashtags are there, condensed, packaged, and delivered from a place of authority. The worst sort of anti-racist workshop simply offers a new language for participants to echo – to retweet out loud.' The dogma is clearly established, and the exchange focuses on how and where somebody knowingly or unknowingly violated it. As Alenka Zupančič noted, the universe of PC workshops is the universe of Brecht's *Jasager*: everybody says yes again and again, and the main argument against those who are not accepted as sincere partisans is 'harm':

> This language, and the framework it expresses, come out of
> the prison-abolition movement. Instead of matching crimes
> with punishments, abolitionists encourage us to think about
> harms and how they can be made right, often through inviting

a broader community to discern the impact of harms, the reasons they came about, and paths forward. In the language of the anti-racism workshop, a harm becomes anything that makes you feel not quite right.

Here is Lloyd's example of how reference to 'harm' works:

> During our discussion of incarceration, an Asian-American student cited federal inmate demographics: About 60 per cent of those incarcerated are white. The black students said they were harmed. They had learned, in one of their workshops, that objective facts are a tool of white supremacy. Outside of the seminar, I was told, the black students had to devote a great deal of time to making right the harm that was inflicted on them by hearing prison statistics that were not about blacks. A few days later, the Asian-American student was expelled from the program.

Two things should surprise us about this story. First, that this new cult combines objectivized dogma with full trust in how one feels (although only the oppressed black students had the right to refer to their feeling as the measure of the racist's guilt). There is no room for a critical confrontation of arguments, the implication being that 'open debate' is a racist white supremacist notion. 'Objective facts are a tool of white supremacy' – yes, so it would follow, as Trumpists used to say, that we need to generate 'alternate facts' . . . To be clear: there is a grain of truth in this position. Those who are brutally oppressed usually have no time to give over to the deep reflection and well-elaborated debate that would bring out the falsity and shortcomings of liberal-humanist ideology. But in this case (as in most other cases), those who have appropriated the role of the leaders of the revolt are precisely not the victims of racist oppression but rather a relatively privileged minority of a minority, participating in a top-quality workshop run by an elite university.

Second, a mystery resides in the functioning of the big Other (the Telluride administrative authority, in this case). The point of view gradually imposed on all participants was the view of a minority (at first, even a minority among the black participants). But how and why did these few succeed in compelling not only their classmates but also the Telluride authorities to take their side, and refuse to defend Lloyd? Why didn't they assume a more nuanced position? More broadly, why does wokeness, although a minority view, succeed in neutralizing the wider liberal and Leftist space, installing in it a fear of critical opposition? Psychoanalysis has a clear answer to this paradox: the notion of *superego*. The superego is a cruel and insatiable agency that bombards me with impossible demands and which mocks my failed attempts to meet them. It is the agency in the eyes of which I am all the more guilty, the more I try to suppress my 'sinful' strivings and meet its demands. The old cynical Stalinist motto about the accused at show trials who professed their innocence ('the more they are innocent, the more they deserve to be shot') is superego at its purest. And did McWhorter in the quoted passage not reproduce the exact structure of the superego-paradox? 'You must strive eternally to understand the experiences of black people / You can never understand what it is to be black, and if you think you do, you're a racist.' In short, you must but you cannot because you shouldn't – the greatest sin is to do what you should strive for . . . This convoluted structure of an injunction which is fulfilled when we fail to meet it accounts for the paradox of superego noted by Freud: the more we obey the superego, the guiltier we feel.

A series of situations that characterize today's society exemplify perfectly this type of superego-pressure, this endless self-examination: was the way I looked at the flight attendant too intrusive and sexually offensive? Did I use any words with a possible sexist undertone? And so on. The pleasure, the thrill even, provided by such self-probing is evident. And does the same not hold even for the pathological fear of some Western liberal Leftists that they may be be guilty of islamophobia? Any critique of Islam is denounced as an expression of Western islamophobia, Salman Rushdie is denounced for unnecessarily provoking Muslims and thus (partially, at least) responsible for the *fatwa* condemning him to death, etc., etc. The result is what one can expect in such cases: the more the Western liberal Leftists probe into their guilt, the more they are accused by Muslim fundamentalists of being hypocrites who try to conceal their hatred of Islam. This constellation again perfectly reproduces the paradox of the superego: the more you obey what the Other demands of you, the guiltier you are. It is as if the more you tolerate Islam, the stronger its pressure on you will be . . .[113]

This superego-structure, then, explains how and why, in the Telluride case, the majority and the institutional big Other were both terrorized by the 'woke' minority. All of them were exposed to a superego-pressure which is far from an authentic call to justice. In such a scenario, the students are fully aware they will not achieve their declared goal of diminishing (at the very least) black oppression, and it is likely that at some level *they even don't want that* – what they really want is what they *are* achieving: a position of moral authority from which to preside over the others without effectively changing the social relations of domination. The situation of the others is more complex, but still clear: they submit to woke discursive demands because most of them really are guilty of participating in social domination, but subscribing to certain ways of talking and thinking offers them an easy way out – you gladly assume your guilt insofar as this enables you to go on living the way you did before. It's the old Protestant logic of 'do whatever you want, just feel guilty for it'.

The lesson of these four examples is thus a clear one: 'Wokeness' effectively stands for its exact opposite. In his *Interpretation of Dreams*, Freud reports on a dream dreamt by a father who falls asleep while keeping guard over his son's coffin; in his dream, his dead son appears to him, pronouncing the terrible appeal 'Father, can't you see that I am burning?' When the father awakens, he discovers that the cloth on the son's coffin has caught fire, one of the burning candles having fallen over. So why did the father awaken? Was it because the smell of the smoke got too strong, meaning it was no longer possible to prolong the sleep by way of including it into the dream? Lacan proposes a much more interesting reading:

> If the function of the dream is to prolong sleep, if the dream, after all, may come so near to the reality that causes it, can we not say that it might correspond to this reality without emerging from sleep? After all, there is such a thing as somnambulistic activity. The question that arises, and which indeed all Freud's previous indications allow us here to produce, is – *What is it that wakes the sleeper?* Is it not, *in* the dream, another reality? – the reality that Freud describes thus – *Dass das Kind an seinem Bette steht*, that the child is near his bed, *ihn am Arme fasst*, takes him by the arm and whispers to him reproachfully, *und ihm vorwurfsvoll zuraunt: Vater, siehst du denn nicht*, Father, can't you see, *dass ich verbrenne*, that I am burning? Is there not more reality in this message than in the noise by which the father also

identifies the strange reality of what is happening in the room next door? Is not the missed reality that caused the death of the child expressed in these words?[114]

So it was not the intrusion of the signal from external reality that awakened the unfortunate father, but the unbearably traumatic character of what he encountered in the dream. Insofar as 'dreaming' means fantasizing in order to avoid confronting the Real, the father literally awakened so that he could go on dreaming. The scenario was the following one: when his sleep was disturbed by the smoke, the father quickly constructed a dream that incorporated the disturbing element (smoke, fire) in order to prolong his sleep; however, what he confronted in the dream was a trauma (of his responsibility for the son's death) much stronger than reality, so he awakened into reality in order to avoid the Real . . . And it is exactly the same with much of the ongoing 'woke' movement: they awaken us (to the horrors of racism and sexism) precisely to enable us to go on sleeping, that is, ignoring the true roots and depth of racial and sexual trauma.

The paradox here is that this sleep is not a passive withdrawal from reality: it functions as frantic activity. How are we to understand this? On today's market, we find a whole series of products deprived of their malignant property: coffee without caffeine, cream without fat, beer without alcohol . . . And the list goes on: virtual sex as sex without sex, the art of expert administration as politics without politics, up to today's tolerant liberal multiculturalism as an experience of other deprived of its disturbing Otherness. We should add to this list another key figure from our cultural space: a *decaffeinated protester*, a sleeping 'woke' protester who says all the right things, but somehow deprives them of their critical edge. He is horrified by global warming and by the war in Ukraine, he fights sexism and racism, he demands radical social change, and everyone is invited to join in, to participate in the big sentiment of global solidarity, which means: you are not required to change your life (perhaps just give to a charity here and there), you go on with your career, you are ruthlessly competitive, but you are on the right side . . . To paraphrase the title of Ben Burgis's book,[115] the agents of cancel culture are 'comedians while the world burns': far from being 'too radical', their imposition of new rules is an exemplary case of pseudo-activity, of how to *make sure that nothing really changes by pretending to act frantically.*

In order to resist the temptations of woke culture, every authentic Leftist should put on the wall above his or her bed or table the opening paragraph of Oscar Wilde's *The Soul of Man under Socialism*, in which he points out that 'it is much more easy to have sympathy with suffering than it is to have sympathy with thought': People

> find themselves surrounded by hideous poverty, by hideous ugliness, by hideous starvation. It is inevitable that they should be strongly moved by all this . . . Accordingly, with admirable, though misdirected intentions, they very seriously and very sentimentally set themselves to the task of remedying the evils that they see. But their remedies do not cure the disease: they merely prolong it. Indeed, their remedies are part of the disease . . . The proper aim is to try and reconstruct society on such a basis that poverty will be impossible. And the altruistic virtues have really prevented the carrying out of this aim . . . It is immoral to use private property in order to alleviate the horrible evils that result from the institution of private property.

The last sentence provides a concise formula of what is wrong with a pan-humanitarian approach, as epitomized by the Bill and

Melinda Gates Foundation. It is not enough just to point out that the Gates charity is based on brutal business practices – one should go a step further and denounce its ideological foundations. The title of Sama Naami's collection of essays, *Refusal of Respect: Why We Should Not Respect Foreign Cultures. Ours Included*,[116] hits the nail on the head: this is the only authentic stance. Gates's charity implies the following variation on Naami's formula: respect all cultures, your own and others. The Rightist nationalist version is: respect your own culture and despise others, which are inferior to it. The politically correct formula is: respect other cultures, but despise your own, which is racist and colonialist (that's why politically correct woke culture is always anti-Eurocentric). The correct Leftist stance is: bring out the hidden antagonisms of your own culture, link it to the antagonisms of other cultures, and then engage in a common struggle between those who fight here, against the oppression and domination at work in our own culture, and those who do the same in other cultures around the world. The words of Lilla Watson, a Murri (Australian Aboriginal) artist and activist, to a rich white compassionate liberal tell it all: 'If you have come here to help me, then don't waste your time. But if you have come here because your liberation is bound up with mine, then come, let us work together.'[117]

What this means is something which may sound shocking, but it is worth insisting on it: you don't have to respect or love immigrants – what you have to do is to change the situation so that they will not have to be immigrants in the first place. The citizen of a developed country who wants to lower immigration levels, and is ready to do something so that migrants don't have to go to a country that they mostly don't even like, is much better than a humanitarian who preaches openness to immigrants while silently participating in the economic and political practices that brought to ruin the countries where the immigrants are coming from. The problem with the ongoing culture wars is that *both* sides ignore this need to change the basic situation, which is why we shouldn't be surprised to find that the reluctance of the American and European new Right (as well as some of the Left) to support Ukraine clearly echoes the Russian position – they are on the same side of the global culture wars.

Russia and Our Culture Wars

A few months into the Russo-Ukrainian war, Jordan Peterson inevitably appeared in some podcasts commenting on it. Although I strongly disagree with his analysis, I think he established a correct link indicated by the title of one of his YouTube videos: 'Russia vs. Ukraine, Or Civil War in the West?'[118] By civil war in the West he of course means the so-called culture wars, the ongoing conflict between the liberal mainstream supporting political correctness and the new populist Right – so how does he relate this to the Ukrainian war?

Although his first move is to strongly condemn the Russian invasion, Peterson's stance gradually morphs into a kind of metaphysical defence of Russia. After enumerating a few carefully selected data points (Ukrainians did curtail some basic rights of the Russian minority, Russia builds new churches, Putin probably is sincerely religious . . .), Peterson focuses on what he considers to be a series of provocations by the US that led Russia to launch its war on Ukraine.

After these preparatory steps, Peterson moves onto his own 'spiritual' topic, resorting to his biggest gun: Dostoyevsky's attack on Western Europe for its hedonist individualism, as opposed to Russian collective spirituality. As expected, Peterson then endorses the Russian designation of today's Western liberal civilization as 'degenerate': postmodernism is a transformation of Marxism,[119] its aim is to destroy the foundations of Christian civilization, so the war in Ukraine is the war of traditional Orthodox Christian values against a new form of Communist degeneracy.

The question to be raised here is: which political force in the West also endorses this Russian vision of the situation? The answer is obvious – the so-called Christian revolt, which made itself unmistakeably apparent for the first time on 6 January 2021. According to CNN, this insurrection 'marked the first time many Americans realized the US is facing a burgeoning White Christian nationalist movement. This movement uses Christian language to cloak sexism and hostility to Black people and non-White immigrants in its quest to create a White Christian America.'[120]

In the Christian nationalist vision, the American nation is divided between 'real Americans' and other citizens who don't deserve the same rights – this was the idea that was used to 'bolster, justify and intensify' the attack on the US Capitol, according to a report by a team of clergy, scholars and advocates. In a survey conducted in 2020 by the Public Religion Research Institute, White evangelical Christians were the group most likely to agree with the statement 'true American patriots might have to resort to violence in order to save the country'. But this stance is not as marginal as you might think: 'White Christian nationalist beliefs have infiltrated the religious mainstream so thoroughly that virtually any conservative Christian pastor who tries to challenge its ideology risks their career,' according to American historian Kristin Kobes Du Mez. Nor is this stance limited just to the US: Viktor Orbán, Peterson's friend, has 'repeatedly lashed out against the 'mixing' of European and non-European races', as the *Guardian* put it.[121] In July 2022, he gave a speech that immediately drew outrage from opposition parties and politicians throughout Europe:

'We [Hungarians] are not a mixed race . . . and we do not want to become a mixed race,' said Orbán. He added that countries where European and non-Europeans mingle were 'no longer nations'.[122]

One cannot but note the irony of the fact that today's Hungarians are themselves a mixed race, the outcome of Huns, intruders from Western Siberia, mixing with local populations. In medieval times, Attila – even today a common Hungarian name – was also called 'the scourge of God', an epithet for any disaster afflicting a nation because of sin. So here we are today, with Orbán playing a new Attila punishing the liberal Europeans for their sins . . . No wonder that, in the ongoing Ukrainian war, Orbán leans towards Russia, while Kaczyński, who shares the same basic view, is resolutely against Russia – but this only proves that we are dealing with a broad coalition stronger than some divides. Who knows, even Ukraine may in the end join this illiberal bloc.

The fact that, after obvious and painful oscillation, Peterson takes this pro-Russian position, is significant as an indication of ongoing global trends. Considering his basic ethical stance, Peterson could easily have taken the opposite position: is the lukewarm response of many Europeans to the war not precisely proof that Europe prefers a fuzzy idea of human rights without firm commitments, that the only 'ethics' it is able to practise is the ethics of self-victimization, of doubting one's own right to act? Would a strong, united response to Russia not be an exemplary case of the stance Peterson advocates in his critique of the Western 'degeneracy'? But this would go against the tide of opinion. The Republican Party lawmakers who oppose support for Ukraine are getting stronger and stronger; they, according to US political website *The Hill*, 'do not want to send money abroad when it can be used in the US to fortify the southern border and invest in domestic energy production, among other issues.'[123] J. D. Vance – the Trump-backed senator for Ohio – criticized Ukraine as a 'corrupt nation run by oligarchs', and while he condemned Russia's invasion, he also called it 'insulting and strategically stupid to devote billions of resources to Ukraine while ignoring the problems in our own country'; Kevin McCarthy, the speaker of the House of Representatives vowed that Republicans would not write a 'blank cheque' for Ukraine.[124]

So we should accept Peterson's basic premise: the Russian attack on Ukraine and the alt-Right revolt in the US are two branches of the same global movement. Does this mean that we should therefore support the opposite side? Here things get complicated. It's true that, if the Western 'Christian revolt' and the Russian anti-European stance unite into one, we will be facing a global socio-political catastrophe with unimaginable implications. However, we are dealing with a familiar antagonism: what Peterson is attacking is the ultimate consequence of global capitalism itself. As Marx and Engels wrote more than 150 years ago in the first chapter of *The Communist Manifesto*:

> The bourgeoisie, wherever it has got the upper hand, has put an end to all feudal, patriarchal, idyllic relations . . . All fixed, fast-frozen relations, with their train of ancient and venerable prejudices and opinions, are swept away, all new-formed ones become antiquated before they can ossify. All that is solid melts into air, all that is holy is profaned, and man is at last compelled to face with sober senses his real conditions of life, and his relations with his kind.[125]

This is ignored by those Leftist cultural theorists who continue to focus their critique on patriarchal ideology and practice. Is it not high time for us to wonder about the fact that the critique of patriarchy has been elevated into a primary target at the very historical moment that it has lost its hegemonic role, when it has been swept away, as Marx and Engels predicted, by market individualism? Such 'Leftists' are, of course, nothing more than clowns in wolves' clothing: posing as radical revolutionaries while defending the establishment.

The culture war raging in the developed West is thus a false war, a war between two versions of the same global capitalist system: its unrestrained, pure market-individualist version and its neo-Fascist conservative version which tries to unite capitalist dynamism with traditional values and liberties. The paradox is here double: Political Correctness is a displacement of good old class struggle – the liberal elite pretends to protect oppressed minority to obfuscate the basic fact of their privileged economic and political position. This lie allows the alt-Right populists to present themselves as a defense of the 'real' working class against the big corporations and the 'deep state' elites. The paradox is thus that today's populist conservatives are more 'revolutionary' than the liberals who are not afraid to call for social order and even police oppression when they feel it is needed ('Where were the police and National Guard on 6 January?'). The implication to be drawn is not that Left and Right are today outdated notions but that both poles of today's cold war can only be properly grasped as a displaced class struggle: neither of them really stands for the exploited.

The solution? Judith Butler, who clearly condemns the Russian attack and also emphasizes the anti-LGBT+ orientation of Russian politics, recently said: 'I am hopeful that the Russian army will lay down its arms.'[126] OK, but what do we do *until* this miracle happens? Simon Tisdall painted a quite accurate picture of what awaits Europe in the near future:

Putin's aim is the immiseration of Europe. By weaponising energy, food, refugees and information, Russia's leader spreads the economic and political pain, creating wartime conditions for all. A long, cold, calamity-filled European winter of power shortages and turmoil looms. Freezing pensioners, hungry youngsters, empty supermarket shelves, unaffordable cost of living increases, devalued wages, strikes and street protests point to Sri Lanka-style meltdowns. An exaggeration? Not really.[127]

One cannot but note how Russian propaganda is painting exactly the same picture of Europe, just attributing it to the Western decay and to Europe's stupid measures against Russia. If we add to this the first signs of the shattering of EU solidarity instigated by Russia (nationwide governments already compete for scarcere sources), the picture gets even clearer: in 'wartime conditions for all', elements of what was once called 'War Communism' will soon become a necessity. The state apparatus, in close coordination with other states and relying on the local mobilization of people, will have to regulate the distribution of energy and food, and prevent the descent of a society into disorder. One should not exclude even a direct intervention of armed forces into social life.

The ongoing crisis offers Europe a choice: our current prospect of 'freezing pensioners, hungry youngsters, empty supermarket shelves, devalued wages, strikes and street protests [pointing] to Sri Lanka-style meltdowns', as Simon Tisdall put it, or mobilization. We have a unique chance to leave behind our pursuit of comfortable, isolated welfarism, whose big worries are, 'How much will gas and electricity prices go up?' and similar concerns. Zelensky recently told *Vogue*. 'Just try to imagine what I'm talking about happening to your home, to your country. Would you still be thinking about gas prices or electricity prices?'[128] He was right: Europe is under attack, so it should mobilize, not just militarily but socially and economically as well. We should use the crisis to change our way of life in a way that will fit our catastrophic ecological predicament and recognize our debt to formerly colonized countries – this is our *only* chance.

Are we ready to do this? I doubt it. But why not? We should reach here beyond the mixture of obvious economic and ideological reasons and focus on a more basic subjective stance that permeates our daily lives: melancholic apathy.

The Disappearance of Interpassivity

As any psychoanalyst will tell you, melancholy precedes prohibition. What makes melancholy so deadening is that objects
of desire are here, available – the subject just no longer desires
them. The function of prohibition is to shatter the subject out
of melancholic lethargy and set alive its desire. If, in melancholy, the object is readily available, while the subject's desire
for it is missing, the wager of prohibition is that, by depriving
the subject of the object, it will resuscitate desire. Today's permissive liberal capitalism is melancholic: we are losing desire
for what we know has to be done. In contrast, nationalist populism mobilizes mourning (for a way of life threatened by
corporate globalization). To make sense of this, James Godley
has evoked Byung-Chul Han's observation that what has made
the pandemic era particularly challenging

> is not just that it [was] harder to participate in mass gatherings,
> but that we no longer even know what such rituals are for. Neo-
> liberal capitalism's valorization of innovative 'disruption' and its
> myopic focus on finding ever new resources for surplus value
> have pathologized these collectivating rituals, replacing them
> with neurotic 'private' ceremonials and confessional experi-
> ences. This has led to stigmatizing structures of collectivity as
> antiquated or even potentially harmful to the social fabric. Thus
> despite, or even because of, the current cultural emphasis on
> openness and interpersonal communication, a subjectivist dis-
> course of psychologization has rerouted concern with objective

social structures to the mental health of individuals. As a result, what has been forgotten, Han observes, is that 'ritual acts also include feelings, but the bearer of these feelings is not the isolated individual' but the community. We have forgotten, for example, how rituals of mourning deal not with individual emotionality but what Han describes as 'an objective feeling, a collective feeling [which] imposes mourning' on everyone collectively and thereby 'consolidate[s] a community'.[129]

In short, proper mourning is only possible when a figure of the big Other – any symbolic authority that sustains a way of life – is doing it for us. We can accept the loss of an object only when this loss is inscribed into the big Other, and unexpected complications can arise when this happens. A friend from Slovenia told me of the tragic end of a young transgender man who wanted to transition legally; he went through all the procedures and, on the day he received official confirmation that he was now recognized by law as a man, he took his own life. It is too easy to speculate about the reasons that may have pushed him to do it (was realizing his deepest desire too much for him?). What we should note is just the weight of the symbolic act: of the inscription of my chosen identity into the official big Other. What drew him to suicide was not any change in his bodily or interpersonal reality (his parents and friends were supportive of his decision) but the mere final step of the state agency registering what he did.

We should recall here the notion of interpassivity (in the authentic sense of this term, developed by Robert Pfaller). Jacques Lacan evokes the common situation of people at a theatre enjoying the performance of a Greek tragedy, but his reading of it makes it clear that something strange is going on: it is as if some figure of the Other (in this case, the Chorus) can take over and experience for us our innermost and most spontaneous feelings and attitudes, inclusive of crying and laughing.[130] In some societies, the same role is played by so-called 'weepers' (women hired to cry at funerals): they can perform the spectacle of mourning for us, relatives of the deceased, allowing us to dedicate our time to more profitable endeavours (like taking care of how to split the inheritance). And what about Tibetan praying wheels? I put a piece of paper with a prayer written on it into the wheel, I mechanically turn it around (or, even more practically, I let the wind turn it around), and the wheel is praying for me. As the Stalinists would have put it, 'objectively' I am praying, even if my thoughts are occupied with the most obscene sexual fantasies. And to dispel the illusion that such things can only happen in 'primitive' societies, think about the so-called 'canned laughter' on a TV-screen (the reaction of laughter to a comic scene which is included into the soundtrack itself): even if I don't laugh and simply stare at the screen, tired after a hard day's work, I nonetheless feel relieved after the show, as if the TV did the laughing for me. To properly grasp this strange process, we need to supplement the fashionable notion of interactivity, with its uncanny double, Pfaller's *interpassivity*.[131] What we get in today's cynical functioning of ideology is interpassive non-knowledge, *the other DOESN'T know for me* – I comfortably dwell in my knowledge, ignoring this knowledge through an Other. This is what happens with today's liberal establishment: as in the 2021 film *Don't Look Up*, they know how things stand (that catastrophe is impending), but they do not act upon this knowledge and transfer their ignorance onto the Other of asteroid deniers.

Is, then, some kind of new prohibition (say, ecologically grounded: a prohibition of activities that endanger our environment) what we need? As Adrian Johnston has put it, 'We know things are broken. We know what needs fixing. We even sometimes have ideas about how to fix them. But, nevertheless, we keep doing nothing either to mend damage already done or to prevent further easily foreseeable damage.'[132]

Where does this passivity come from? Today's global capitalism generates apathy precisely because it demands from us permanent hyper-activity, constant engagement in its devastating dynamic – are we aware how thoroughly our daily lives have changed in the last few decades? So, to open up the path for a real change, we have first to put a brake on the mad rhythm of continuous change. We are never given a moment of respite to think. Apathy is thus the other side of extreme dynamism: things change all the time to make sure that nothing that matters really changes. It's a little bit like the compulsive neurotic – like me – who talks and gesticulates all the time not to achieve something but because he is afraid that, if he stops for a moment, others will notice the worthlessness of what he is doing and may raise a question that really matters.

This stuckness, sustained by hyper-activity, also allows us to explain how today's capitalism succeeds in neutralizing threats and critical voices to a degree unthinkable for Marx. Today, ideology functions less and less like a symptom and more and more like a fetish. Symptomal functioning makes ideology vulnerable to ideologico-critical procedure: in the classic Enlightenment way, when an individual caught in ideology understands the hidden mechanism of ideological deception, the symptom disappears, the spell of ideology is broken. In the fetishist functioning, ideology works in a cynical mode, it includes a distance towards itself – or, to repeat Sloterdijk's old formula of cynical reason: 'I know what I am doing, but I am nonetheless doing it.' As Alenka Zupančič wrote, in a cynical mode, the fetishist disavowal 'I know very well, but . . . (I don't really believe it)' is raised to a higher reflexive level: fetish is not the element to which I hold so that I can act while ignoring what I know – fetish is *this knowledge itself.* The cynical reasoning is: 'I know very well what I'm doing, so you cannot reproach me that I don't know what I am doing.' This is how, in today's capitalism, hegemonic ideology includes (and thereby neutralizes the efficiency of) critical knowledge: critical distance towards the social order is the very medium through which this order reproduces itself. Just think about today's explosion of art biennales (Venice, Kassel . . .): although they usually present themselves as a form of resistance towards global capitalism and its commodification of everything, they are in their mode of organization the ultimate form of art as a moment of capitalist self-reproduction.

When the public space of mourning disintegrates into neurotic private ceremonials and confessional experiences, social space is still here, it is just no longer the big Other of rituals and unwritten rules but a privately owned space for the direct exchange of private obscenities – like Zuckerberg's metaverse. What this means is that, at this very moment when we are helping Ukrainians to defend freedom, we should be more attentive than ever to what true freedom is. The finale of Act I of Mozart's *Don Giovanni* begins with don Giovanni's powerful appeal, '*Viva la libertà!*', repeated forcefully by all, interrupting the melodic flow, as if the music gets stuck at this point of excessive engagement. But the catch is, of course, that, although the entire group is enthusiastically unified around the call to freedom, each subgroup projects into '*liberta*' its own dreams and hopes, or, to quote Étienne Balibar: 'Sociability is therefore the unity of a real agreement and an imaginary ambivalence, both of which have real effects.'[133]

Imagine a situation of political unity where all sides unite under the same Master-signifier ('freedom'), but every particular group projects a different meaning into this universality (freedom of property for some, anarchic freedom outside the state law for others, social conditions which allow individuals to actualize their potentials for yet another group, and so on). The contours of freedom are, of course, historically variable, which brings us to the profound historicity of the predominant notion of freedom: to simplify it to the utmost, in traditional societies freedom does not refer to equality – freedom means that each person should be free to play his or her specific role in the hierarchic order. In modern societies, freedom is linked to abstract legal equality and personal liberty (a poor worker and his rich employer are equally free); from the mid-nineteenth century, freedom is more and more linked to those social circumstances that enable me to actualize it (minimal welfare, free education, healthcare, etc.). Today, the accent is on 'freedom of choice', which implies that we ignore how the very frame of choices is imposed on individuals, which choices are *de facto* privileged, etc. Freedom begins with questioning its own frame. Now, in Ukraine, everyone is crying *'Viva la libertà!'*, but if – or, more hopefully, when – they succeed in their struggle, they will face the true choice: which freedom should they finally enjoy? Should they just try to catch up with Western liberal democracy, which is itself in crisis? Should they join the conservative–populist axis of Poland and Hungary? Or will they realize they have to find a new way? The structure of our political space does appear to be changing, but not to something truly 'new'. The big shift is that the opposition between centre-Left and centre-Right parties as the main axis of our political space has been replaced by the opposition between big technocratic parties (standing for expert knowledge) and populist opponents with anti-corporate and anti-financial motifs. However, this shift itself has undergone another surprising turn: what we have been witnessing lately is something one cannot but describe as techno-populism: a political movement with clear populist appeal (working for the people as such, for their 'real interests', 'neither Left nor Right'), promising to take care of the people through rational expert politics, a matter-of-fact approach, without mobilizing low passions and resorting to demagogic slogans. To quote Christopher Bickerton and Carlo Accetti:

> Technocratic appeals to expertise and populist invocations of 'the people' have become mainstays of political competition in established democracies. This development is best understood as the emergence of techno-populism – a new political logic that is being superimposed on the traditional struggle between left and right. Political movements and actors combine technocratic and populist appeals in a variety of ways, as do more established parties that are adapting to the particular set of incentives and constraints implicit in this new, unmediated form of politics.[134]

What seemed the ultimate antagonism of today's politics, the big struggle between liberal democracy and Rightist nationalist populism, has thus miraculously transformed into a peaceful coexistence – are we dealing here with some kind of 'dialectical synthesis' of opposites? No, because the opposites are reconciled through the exclusion of the third term: the political antagonism, i.e., the political dimension as such. The unsurpassed model here was Mario Draghi in Italy, who was endorsed as the 'neutral' and efficient prime minister by the entire political spectrum (with the significant exception of the extreme Rightist neo-Fascists, who are saving the honour of politics), but elements of techno-populism are clearly recognizable also in Emmanuel Macron and even in Angela Merkel.

The embarrassing paradox we are compelled to accept is that, from the moral standpoint, the most comfortable way to maintain one's moral high ground is to live in a moderately authoritarian regime. One can softly (following the unwritten rules) oppose the regime (without really posing a threat to it), so that one can be assured of one's upright moral stance without risking a lot. Even if one does suffer some disadvantages (some jobs are out of reach, one can be prosecuted), such minor punishments only provide the aura of a hero. But once full democracy comes, we all enter the domain of disorientation: choices are no longer so clear. For example, in Hungary in the mid-1990s, the liberal ex-dissidents had to make a difficult choice: should they enter into a coalition with ex-Communists to prevent the conservative Right taking power? This was a strategic decision where simple moral reasoning was not enough. That's why so many political agents in post-Socialist countries long for the old times when choices were clear – in despair, they try to return to the old clarity by equating their actual opponent with old Communists. In Slovenia conservative nationalists still blame ex-Communists for all the country's present troubles – for example, they claim that the high number of anti-vaxxers is the result of a continuing Communist legacy; at the same time, Left liberals claim that, while they were in power, the conservative nationalists governed in exactly the same authoritarian way as the Communists did before 1990. The first gesture of a new politics must be this: to fully admit disorientation and to assume the responsibility for difficult strategic choices.

So parliamentary democracy as we know it is more and

more unable to resolve the problems we are facing. However, if we just avoid 'false' solutions and wait for the right moment, it will never come – time is against us, and we have to engage ourselves in whatever way possible, with the hope that even failure would lay the foundations for further changes. The Syriza movement in Greece didn't come to power just with elections: it arose out of a vast tapestry of civil-society protest groups and years of mobilization – the tragedy was that, after the victory of Syriza, this tapestry disintegrated. Here we again stumble upon the question which haunts this book: how do we achieve a real change in an epoch when what the media present as progress is most often a retreat masked as a step forwards?

Tax the Rich? Not Enough!

In politics, *larvatus prodeo* ('I go forward masked') is often quite appropriate: a revolutionary force, when it takes over, often at first does not show its true colours and just claims it wants to make the existing system better. But is it not even more appropriate to turn the saying around: *larvatus redeo*? When I am forced to retreat, I assume a deceiving mask, to cover up the depth of my defeat and present it as progress . . . However, what if the naked face itself is already a mask, so that when I retreat, I pretend to drop my mask and offer my true face – which is the ultimate deception. Just recall politicians who (often late in their age) betray their radical roots and claim that they are now no longer possessed by false visions: 'I renounce my ideological illusions, now I am just who I truly am.'

This version of *larvatus redeo* perfectly fits the fetishist functioning of ideology in its cynical mode, which includes a distance towards itself – or, to repeat Peter Sloterdijk's old formula of cynical reason: 'I know what I am doing, but I am nonetheless doing it.' The fetishist disavowal 'I know very well, but . . . (I don't really believe it)' is thus raised to a higher reflexive level: fetish is not the element to which I hold so that I can act ignoring what I know – fetish is *this knowledge itself*. Recall the big conference about climate change in Glasgow two years ago: the urgent need for global cooperation and green action was publicly embraced, but all this declarative blahblah had no real effect. And it is quite probable that the same will happen with anti-capitalist talk: very little will really change; any threat to the system will be effectively neutralized.

The predominant critical stance in our big media still avoids capitalism. Here is an exemplary case. Harry and Meghan have joined Ethic, a company that invests in sustainable projects, as 'impact officers' – Ethic's website says: 'They're deeply committed to helping address the defining issues of our time – such as climate, gender equity, health, racial justice, human rights, and strengthening democracy – and understand that these issues are inherently interconnected.'[135] One cannot but note that something is missing in this list of the 'defining issues of our time': yes, these issues are 'inherently interconnected', but not directly – what mediates their connection is global capitalism and its destructive effects.

Against this predominant stance, a version of direct anti-capitalism is gradually spreading even in our mainstream media. It began a decade or more ago with what one cannot but call Hollywood-Marxism, from movies like *Avatar*, which transposes class struggle into a conflict between alien organic-patriarchal culture living in harmony with nature on one hand and brutal corporate capitalism trying to colonize and exploit them on the other, up to killing-the-rich movies (*Glass Onion, Menu, Triangle of Sadness* . . .). Similarly, economic debates are first constrained to the critique of ultra-rich: many members of this elite are calling on governments to tax them more in order to help billions of people who struggle to survive. We recently learned that '2 per cent of Elon Musk's wealth could solve world hunger'[136] – and Musk (who recently lost over half of his wealth, around $160 billion) immediately offered the money if the UN could propose a clear model of how to achieve the goal . . . While 'tax the rich' is something to enact, we should nonetheless bear in mind that it leaves the basic functioning of the system intact, while just trying to constrain its excesses. Even some big media are becoming aware that more is needed – the *Financial Times* declared in an editorial that neoliberalism has to descend from the global scene since its time has passed: the capitalist dynamic more and more looks like a hamster running in the wheel of its cage.[137]

So what is needed? The first thing to do is to learn to cross the red lines imposed by neoliberal ideology: today's capitalism can survive much more radical interventions than may appear possible. Mariana Mazzucato pointed out that the system that constantly repeated the mantra that we cannot raise taxes to fight global warming was able to spend trillions to combat the omicron epidemic.[138] So we should begin by courageously strengthening what Peter Sloterdijk called 'objective Social Democracy': the true triumph of Social Democracy occurred when its basic demands (free education and healthcare, etc.) became part of the programme accepted by all main parties and were inscribed into the functioning of the state institutions themselves.

But this will not be enough. The second thing to do is to become aware that the existing multi-party parliamentary system is not effective enough to cope with the crises that beset us. We shouldnt fetishize multi-party parliamentary democracy – what Friedrich Engels wrote in a letter to August Bebel from 1884 still holds. Engels warned that 'pure democracy' often becomes a slogan for counter-revolutionary reaction: 'At the moment of revolution, the entire reactionary mass will act as though they were democrats . . . At all events, on the crucial day and the day after, they will act as though they were democrats.'[139] Does exactly this not happen when an emancipatory movement in power gets too radical? Was not – among many others – the coup against Evo Morales in Bolivia done on behalf of democracy?

Lenin observed (from a balcony overlooking the hall) the last session of the Russian Constituent Assembly, on 5 January 1918. Afterwards, the Assembly was *de facto* disbanded, never convoked again – democracy (in the usual sense of the word, at least) was over in Russia, since this Assembly was the last multiparty elected body. Here is Lenin's reaction which is worth a longer quote:

'Friends, I have lost a day,' says an old Latin tag. One cannot help but recall it when one remembers how the fifth of January was lost.

After real, lively, Soviet work among workers and peasants engaged on *real tasks*, clearing the forest and uprooting the stumps of landowner and capitalist exploitation, we were suddenly transported to 'another world', to arrivals from another world, from the camp of the bourgeoisie with its willing or unwilling, conscious or unconscious champions, with its hangers-on, servants and advocates. Out of the world in which the working people and their Soviet organization were conducting the struggle against the exploiters we were transported to the world of saccharine phrases, of slick, empty declamations, of promises and more promises based, as before, on conciliation with the capitalists.

It is as though history had accidentally, or by mistake, turned its clock back, and January 1918 for a single day became May or June 1917!

It was terrible! To be transported from the world of living people into the company of corpses, to breathe the odor of the dead, to hear those mummies with their empty 'social' Louis Blanc phrases, was simply intolerable . . .

It was a hard, boring and irksome day in the elegant rooms of the Taurida Palace, whose very aspect differs from that of

Smolny approximately in the same way as elegant, but moribund bourgeois parliamentarism differs from the plain, proletarian Soviet apparatus that is in many ways still disorderly and imperfect but is living and vital. There, in that old world of bourgeois parliamentarism, the leaders of hostile classes and hostile groups of the bourgeoisie did their *fencing*. Here, in the new world of the proletarian and peasant, socialist state, the oppressed classes are making clumsy, inefficient . . . [manuscript breaks off at this point][140]

It is, of course, easy to mock the quoted passage, seeing in it just the first step towards the Stalinist dictatorship, and to strike back: what about the meetings and debates within the Bolshevik party itself? Did they not in a couple of years also turn into 'the world of saccharine phrases, of slick, empty declamations,' a world of empty rituals in which members also acted like zombies, and in which one could also 'breathe the odour of the dead'? But, on the other hand, does Lenin's brutally icy description not fit perfectly big meetings about global warming like the Glasgow conference, which also transport us 'to the world of saccharine phrases . . . of promises and more promises based, as before, on conciliation with the capitalists'?

In search of a different democracy, one is tempted to turn to today's China. Roland Boer did this,[141] arguing that, while China is not simply a global model for all of us to follow, it provides useful lessons, since it shows how to combine economic growth and a strong role for the market with socialism. The complex development from Deng Hsiao Ping's reforms to Xi Jinping's new vision cannot be reduced to a conflict between (a limited dose of) market capitalism and Communist 'totalitarianism', as the usual Western 'democratic' critique suggests. Xi repeatedly insists that the task is to redirect the growth so that ordinary poor people will feel the benefits, and he emphasizes the public control over markets. That's why the leading role of the Communist party is needed: it guarantees that the dynamic of the big capital is directed towards the common good of the majority, the rights of women and minorities, as well as towards keeping in check threats to our environment . . .

So is China showing the way? Not quite: the public unrest that triggered the turnaround in the struggle against Covid was just one among many signs that the ruling elite does not effectively register and react to ordinary people's discontents. Behind the proclaimed goal of closely listening to the discontent and the demands of the majority, lurks a society in which public media are tightly controlled and censored; plus, the way the Party leadership is selected is far from transparent.

On the other hand, the explosive rise of the new media (Facebook, Google, Instagram, TikTok, etc.) in the 'democratic' West radically changed the relationship between public and private space: a new third space has emerged that violates the division between public and private. This new space is public, globally accessible; but it simultaneously functions as an exchange of private messages. It is far from being uncontrolled: there are algorithms that not only censor it, preventing some messages from entering it, but also manipulate the way messages catch our attention. The task is here to move beyond the alternative 'China or Elon Musk': neither the non-transparent state control nor the 'freedom' to do what one wants that is also manipulated by non-transparent algorithms. What China and Musk share is the non-transparent control by algorithms.

What we need is almost self-evident: of course we need algorithms that control access (preventing racist and sexist content, etc.), but these algorithms should be totally transparent, publicly debated and fully accessible. Some theorists think that, with this new space, the very notion of ideology is no longer of any use – but it is easy to show that ideology remains fully operative here: the 'freedom' we enjoy in this space is an exemplary mode of un-freedom experienced as freedom, of freedom which is tightly regulated, manipulated and controlled. In his 'Foreword' to Søren Mau's *Mute Compulsion*, Michael Heinrich points out how the term 'mute compulsion', used by Marx a couple of times in his *Capital*, is 'of central importance in the contrast between personal relations of domination such as slavery or serfdom in pre-capitalist modes of production, and the impersonal domination of legally free wage labourers by which Marx characterizes the capitalist mode of production'. This notion is thus

> a key component of the specifically economic 'power of capital', a power based on altering the material conditions of social reproduction. For his examination of the question, already much discussed, of how capitalist relations repeatedly reproduce themselves despite all crises and contradictions, Søren had named a third type of power relations alongside those based on violence and those based on ideology. While the first two have a direct effect on people, this third type asserts itself indirectly by reshaping people's economic and social environment.[142]

The only point I am tempted to disagree with here is the distinction between mute compulsion and ideology: this distinction holds only if we conceive of ideology in the narrow sense of explicit legal and notional constructs. However, I think that, in our (wrongly) so-called 'post-ideological' era, the main space in which ideology remains fully operative is precisely the thick network of daily practices with their implicit rules and customs that we follow without even being fully aware of them – the domain, precisely, of 'mute ideology'.

The third thing: the focus on 'real' economic problems is also not enough: we will be forced to fully absorb the lessons of psychoanalysis. Friedrich Engels wrote that in socialism 'the satisfaction of all reasonable needs will be assured to everyone in an ever-increasing measure',[143] but one should raise the inevitable question: what, precisely, are these 'reasonable needs'? Isn't the big lesson of psychoanalysis that, in our social universe, needs are never directly expressed: they are always mediated by psychic mechanisms that make them perverted 'irrational' desires? I am ready to risk my life for something that I don't need; the prohibition of directly getting what I desire can itself provide surplus-pleasure; what I desire is mediated by what others desire; there is the mechanism of envy that makes it more important to hurt the other than to satisfy myself . . . How can one explain things like racism and sexism without such perverted reversals? Fredric Jameson pointed out that, if we imagine some kind of communism, envy will be its basic problem. So the passage to (whatever version of) post-capitalism will be not only a very complex process at the level of the economy, it will also confront us with new problems of libidinal economy – the ultimate lesson is, 'no critique of political economy without a critique of libidinal economy'. And we are not talking here just about supplementing a critique of political economy with a critique of libidinal economy: a close reading of Marx shows that a kind of critique of libidinal economy is already present in his *Capital*. Does Marx not characterize capitalism as a system run by an incessant drive (*Trieb*) towards expanded self-reproduction?

The conclusion is thus that one should not cynically dismiss the emerging critiques of capitalism: they have opened up a new space of critical thinking, and it is up to us whether this space will be recaptured by the system or not. To avoid this recapture, the first thing to do is to fully assume the fact that it is not enough to tell the truth: one has to tell it in a way that mobilizes people to act on it, not to indulge in self-righteous satisfaction. Why? Friedrich Jacobi, the German philosopher active around 1800, wrote: *'La verité en la repoussant, on l'embrasse'* ('In repelling the truth, one embraces it'). Examples of this paradox abound – for example, the Enlightenment really won against traditional faith and authority when the partisans of the traditional view began to use Enlightenment rational argumentation to justify their stance (a society needs firm unquestionable authority to enjoy a stable life, etc.). But does the same hold also the opposite way? Is it that in embracing the truth one repels it? This is exactly what is happening today: 'truth' (the urgent need for global co-operation, etc.) is repelled by the public embracing of the need for green action, for collaborative action to fight pandemic, as happened in the Glasgow conference mentioned earlier. This mechanism was already being described back in 1937 by George Orwell, who deployed the ambiguity of the predominant Leftist attitude towards class differences:

> We all rail against class-distinctions, but very few people ser-iously want to abolish them. Here you come upon the important fact that every revolutionary opinion draws part of its strength from a secret conviction that nothing can be changed . . . So long as it is merely a question of ameliorating the worker's lot, every decent person is agreed. . . . But unfortunately you get no further by merely wishing class-distinctions away. More exactly, it *is* necessary to wish them away, but your wish has no efficacy unless you grasp what it involves. The fact that has got to be faced is that to abolish class-distinctions means abolishing a part of yourself . . . I have got to alter myself so completely that at the end I should hardly be recognizable as the same person.[144]

Orwell's point is that radicals invoke the need for revolutionary change as a kind of superstitious token that should achieve the opposite, i.e. *prevent* the change from really occurring – today's academic Leftists who criticize capitalist cultural imperialism are in reality horrified at the thought of their field of study really breaking down. And the same goes for our fight against the pandemic and global warming – a paraphrase of Orwell is appropriate here:

> We all rail against global warming and the pandemic, but very few people seriously want to abolish them. So long as it is merely a question of ameliorating the lot of ordinary people, every decent person is agreed. But unfortunately you get no further by merely wishing global warming and the pandemic away. More exactly, it *is* necessary to wish them away, but your wish has no efficacy unless you grasp what it involves. The fact that has got to be faced is that to abolish global warming and the pandemic means abolishing a part of yourself. Each of us will have to alter him/herself so completely that at the end s/he will hardly be recognizable as the same person.

Are we ready for this? The answer is an obvious NO. To quote again from Adrian Johnston: 'We know things are broken. We know what needs fixing. We even sometimes have ideas about how to fix them. But, nevertheless, we keep doing nothing either to mend damage already done or to prevent fur-ther easily foreseeable damage.'[145] Where does this passivity come from? Take the pandemic as a case in point. Our media often speculate which hidden motives make anti-vaxxers so adamantly persist in their stance, but, as far as I know, they never evoke the most obvious reason: at some level they *desire* a continuation of the pandemic, and they know that refusing anti-pandemic measures will prolong it. If this is the case, then the next question to be raised is: what (which feature) makes the anti-vaxxers desire the continuation of the pandemic?

We should avoid here not only any pseudo-Freudian notions like some version of death-drive, of a wish to suffer and die. The idea that anti-vaxxers oppose anti-pandemic measures because they are not ready to sacrifice the Western-liberal way of life which is for them the only possible frame of freedom and dignity is true, but not enough. We should add here a perverse enjoyment in the very renunciation of ordinary pleasures that the pandemic brings about. We should not underestimate the secret satisfaction provided by the passive life of depression and apathy, of just dragging on without a clear life-project.

However, the change that is required is not just a subjective one but a global social change. At the beginning of the pandemic, I wrote that the disease would deal a mortal blow to capitalism. I referred to the final scene of Tarantino's *Kill Bill 2*, in which Beatrix disables the evil Bill and strikes him with the 'Five Point Palm Exploding Heart Technique', a combination of five strikes with one's fingertips to five different pressure points on the target's body – after the target walks away and has taken five steps, their heart explodes in their body and they fall to the ground. My point was that the coronavirus epidemic was a kind of 'Five Point Palm Exploding Heart Technique' attack on the global capitalist system – a signal that we cannot go on the way we were up until now, that a radical change is needed.

Many people laughed at me afterwards: capitalism not only contained the crisis but even exploited it to strengthen itself . . . I still think I was right. In the last years, global capitalism has changed so radically that some (such as Yanis Varoufakis and Jodi Dean) no longer even call the new emerging order capitalism but, rather, 'corporate neo-feudalism'. The pandemic gave a boost to this new corporate order, with new feudal lords like Bill Gates or Mark Zuckerberg more and more controlling our common spaces of communication and exchange.

The pessimistic conclusion that imposes itself is that even stronger shocks and crises will be needed to awaken us. Neoliberal capitalism is already dying, so the forthcoming battle will not be the one between neoliberalism and its beyond but the one between two forms of this beyond: corporate neo-feudalism, which promises protective bubbles against the threats (like Zuckerberg's 'metaverse'), bubbles in which we can continue to dream, and the rude awakening which will compel us to invent new forms of solidarity. At this point in time, this solidarity has a name: it is embodied in one person rotting in a London jail without being accused of anything: Julian Assange.

Assange: Yes, We Can!

In January 2022, the British High Court ruled that Julian Assange could be extradited from the UK to the US; the US thus won its appeal against an earlier ruling that had blocked his extradition on the grounds that the risks to his mental health were too great. This last twist in the endless Assange saga was just the culmination of a long and slow well-orchestrated campaign of character assassination which had reached the lowest level imaginable a few years previously, when unverified rumours began to circulate that Ecuadorians in the London embassy wanted rid of him because of his bad smell and dirty clothes.

In the first stage of attacks on Assange, his former friends and collaborators went public with claims that WikiLeaks began its work with good intentions but then got bogged down in Assange's political bias (his anti-Hillary obsession, his suspicious ties with Russia . . .). This was followed by more direct personal defamation: he was called paranoiac and arrogant, obsessed by power and control.[146] Then we reached the most intimate, direct line of attack: bodily smells and stains.[147] The only thing that really smelled bad, though, was the response of some mainstream feminists who refused any solidarity with Assange on the basis that they would offer no help to rapists.[148] (Assange was accused of rape in Sweden, but the charges have since been dropped on the basis of insufficient evidence.) In this case, a – to say the least – very suspicious accusation, which never even became a formal charge, outweighted the fact of being a victim of state terror.

Assange, a paranoiac? When you live permanently in an apartment which is bugged from above and below, a victim of constant surveillance organized by secret services, who wouldn't be paranoid? Megalomaniac? When the (now ex-) head of the CIA says your arrest is his priority, does not this imply that you are a 'big' threat to at least some people? Behaving like the head of a spy organization? But WikiLeaks *is* a spy organization, although one that serves the people, keeping them informed of what goes on behind the scenes. So why is Assange such a traumatic figure for the establishment? Where does this ridiculously excessive desire for revenge stem from? What did Assange, his colleagues, and whistleblowing sources do to deserve this? In a way, one can understand the authorities: Assange and colleagues like Snowden are often accused of being traitors, but they are something much worse (in the eyes of the authorities). As Alenka Zupančič put it, the problem is that they are not playing the usual 'patriotic games' and selling information to other intelligence services:

> we are dealing with something entirely different. We are dealing with a gesture which questions the very logic, the very status quo, which for quite some time has served as the only foundation of all 'Western' (non-)politics. With a gesture which as it were risks everything, with no consideration of profit and without its own stakes: it takes the risk because it is based on the conclusion that what is going on is simply wrong. Snowden didn't propose any alternative. Snowden, or, rather, the logic of his gesture, like, say, before him, the gesture of Bradley Manning – *is* the alternative.[149]

This breakthrough of WikiLeaks is nicely encapsulated by Assange's ironic self-designation as a 'spy for the people':

spying for the people is not a direct negation of spying (which would rather be acting as a double agent, selling our secrets to the enemy); it undermines the very universal principle of spying, the principle of secrecy, since its goal is to make secrets public. But there is a deeper reason Assange causes such unease: he has made it clear that the most dangerous threat to freedom does not come from an openly authoritarian power, it takes place when our unfreedom itself is experienced as freedom – how?

Is there anything more 'free' than our browsing on the web, searching for the topics we like? However, most of our activities (and passivities) are now registered in some digital cloud which also permanently evaluates us, tracing not only our acts but also our emotional states; when we experience ourselves as free to the utmost (surfing the web, where everything is available), we are totally 'externalized' and subtly manipulated. The digital network gives new meaning to the old slogan, 'the personal is political'. And it's not only the control of our intimate lives that is at stake: everything is today regulated by some digital network, from transport to health, from electricity to water. That's why the web is our most important commons today, and the struggle for its control is *the* struggle today. The enemy is the combination of privatized and state-controlled commons, corporations (Google, Facebook) and state security agencies (NSA).

Take the case of Bill Gates: how did he become one of the richest men in the world? His wealth has nothing to do with efficient production costs or canny pricing (and one could even argue that Microsoft pays its intellectual workers relatively high salaries) – in other words, Microsoft isn't that much cheaper or better than its competitors. Why, then, are millions still buying it? Because Microsoft has imposed itself as an almost universal standard, (almost) monopolizing the field. Things are similar with Jeff Bezos and Amazon, with Apple, with Facebook, and so on. In all these cases, the commons themselves – the platforms (spaces of social exchange and interaction) – have been privatized, which puts us, their users, into the position of serfs paying a rent to the owner of a common as our feudal master.

Wealth and power are increasingly concentrated in the hands of a few dizzyingly influential men. With regard to Facebook, Mark Zuckerberg 'has unilateral control over 3 billion people' due to his unassailable position at the top of Facebook, the whistleblower Frances Haugen told British MPs in 2021, as she called for urgent external regulation to rein in the tech company's management and reduce the harm being done to society.[150] The big achievement of modernity, the public square, is thus disappearing. Days after the Haugen revelations, Zuckerberg announced that his company would change its name from 'Facebook' to 'Meta', and outlined his vision of the 'metaverse' in a speech that was a true neo-feudal manifesto. As CNN reported,

> Zuckerberg wants the metaverse to ultimately encompass the rest of our reality – connecting bits of real space here to real space there, while totally subsuming what we think of as the real world. In the virtual and augmented future Facebook has planned for us, it's not that Zuckerberg's simulations will rise to the level of reality, it's that our behaviors and interactions will become so standardized and mechanical that it won't even matter. Instead of making human facial expressions, our avatars can make iconic thumbs-up gestures. Instead of sharing air and space together, we can collaborate on a digital document. We learn to downgrade our experience of being together with

another human being to seeing their projection overlaid into the room like an augmented reality Pokemon figure.[151]

The metaverse is intended to act as a virtual space beyond (*meta*) our fractured and hurtful reality, a virtual space in which we will smoothly interact through our avatars, with elements of augmented reality (reality overlaid with digital signs). It thus aims to be nothing less than meta-physics actualized: a meta-physical space fully subsuming reality, which will be allowed to enter it in fragments only insofar as it will be overlaid by digital guidelines manipulating our perception and intervention. And the catch is familiar: we end up with a commons that is privately owned, with a private feudal lord overseeing and regulating our interaction.

But this is not all: the threat to our freedom disclosed by whistleblowers has even deeper systemic roots. Assange should be defended not just because his acts embarrassed the US secret services, but because he has revealed that all other great (and not so great) powers (from China to Russia, from Germany to Israel) are guilty of doing the same thing, too (to the extent that they are technologically cable of doing it). Assange's acts have thus provided a factual foundation to our premonition that we are all monitored and controlled. The lesson is global; it reaches far beyond the US. We didn't really learn from Assange (or Snowden or Manning) anything we didn't already presume to be true – but it is one thing to know it in general, and another to get concrete data. It is a little bit like knowing that one's sexual partner is playing around – one can accept the abstract knowledge of it, but pain arises when one hears the details of what they were doing . . .

Now we have reached the core of the entire affair. The true target of Assange's revelations is us: average, hypocritical liberals who are well aware what state apparatuses and big companies do discreetly, but prefer to ignore it. Publicly we protest, at least from time to time, but silently we know that somebody has to do the dirty job discreetly. Assange blocks this way out: he compels us to publicly assume the knowledge we prefer to ignore. In this sense, Assange is fighting for us, against our complacency, the complacency which also explains why there is still no large movement in support of Assange, why very few 'big names' (like movie stars, writers or journalists) are ready to defend him. This is the complacency that enables those in power to ignore us still.

Conclusion: How Do We Begin When It's Too Late?

So, for the third and last time, what is to do be done? We always, by definition, begin to solve a problem too late – for a simple reason: the only alternative would have been to prevent the problem from arising in the first place, in the past. Yes, we should fight racism, but we can only do so after allowing racism to arise, and so our struggle against it always comes too late. There is no place here for a cheap historicism that relativizes the injustice: it's not that things that were once 'normal' (slavery, racism, sexual oppression) are now unacceptable because our culture and sensitivities have changed. We should do precisely what historicist relativization forbids: we should measure the past with today's standards. Once we see that slavery is wrong, we simultaneously see that it was *always* wrong, and become able to read history differently, discovering – for example – how slave revolts happened all the time.

So what should we do now, when it's too late? Unique opportunities for action arise all the time – opportunities not just to do the best possible thing in a given situation but to change the very coordinates of the situation itself. I am writing these lines on the first anniversary of the Russian attack on Ukraine. The first thing to do on this day is to recognize and celebrate the Ukrainian resistance which surprised everyone, including their allies, and maybe even many Ukrainians themselves. Linked to this is another positive change in Ukraine, as Kateryna Semchuk has reported:

people's desire for justice at home has not diminished. If anything, it has got stronger – and rightly so, since most citizens are risking their lives to fight the genocidal threat posed by Russia. People have such a personal stake in Ukraine's future, they are more sensitive than ever about what kind of country we are becoming, and how things should be after the war.[152]

Let's hope that the ongoing anti-corruption campaign will grow into a more radical questioning about 'how things should be after the war': should Ukraine simply catch up with Western liberal democracy and accept being economically colonized by big Western corporations? Will it join the neo-conservative backlash, as Poland did? Will it risk trying to resuscitate the old social democracy? This moment offers the possibility for a true act: not just to repel Russian aggression but to use it to set in motion a radical social transformation.

Another aspect that has to be noted are the international repercussions of the Russian invasion: to really condemn Russia's colonialism, we should consider Ukraine alongside other neocolonial cases, like that of Israel and Palestine. It is true that Israel is not occupying the West Bank as the result of an invasion but after the 1967 war, which the Arab nations lost, and that its regime of military occupation has lasted for over half a century. But the fact that the large majority of West Bank Palestinians were born under occupation, without a clear prospect of gaining some kind of statehood, and forced to helplessly watch as their land gets gradually appropriated by Jewish settlers, makes their resistance more than understandable. But still, while our media are full of praise for Ukraine's 'heroic resistance', solidarity with those West Bank Palestinians who resist the expansion of illegal settlements is rare. Generally, as we have seen, such solidarity is instantly denounced as anti-Semitic.

But now, with the new Israeli government engaged in the *de facto* annexation of the West Bank, the parallel with Russia has become much more pertinent. In December 2022, the government stated that the Jewish people have an 'exclusive and indisputable right to *all parts* of the Land of Israel' (which, according to the Jewish tradition, was promised to the Jewish people by God, and includes Judea and Samaria, or the West Bank). It further declared that 'Israeli sovereignty shall be applied to the West Bank,' plus it announced the change 'from the law of occupation to an application of Israeli domestic law', that is, annexation in all but name. What this means is, among other things, a 'change to the enemy property law which will "release" property in the West Bank that was held by Israelis prior to 1948 back into their hands.'[153] (But why not the same for Palestinian properties in Israel?)

In principle, such a change could be a progressive act, since it implies that 'there can no longer be justification for application of different legal regimes to Israelis and West Bank Palestinians.' However, Israel will be faced with a problem here: if the West Bank simply becomes part of Israel, what to do with the well over two million Palestinians living on the West Bank? If they are made regular Israeli citizens, they will form together with today's Israeli Palestinians a very strong voting bloc, which is for sure unacceptable to the present Israeli government. (Therein resides, also, the true reason why Israel has not already annexed the West Bank.) How to prevent this? There are only two options: either eject from Israel as many Palestinians as possible, or impose 'an institutionalized regime of systematic oppression and domination by one racial group over another, with the intention of maintaining this regime, otherwise known as apartheid'.[154]

So, in today's Israel, what would a true political act look like? Since the beginning of 2023 the country has been shaken by demonstrations against the new Rightist government and its brutal politics which, among other things, proposes to subordinate the independent judiciary to political power. However, these hundreds of thousands of liberal, freedom-loving protesters have more or less totally ignored the plight of the Palestinians (20 per cent of the population) who will obviously suffer most from the new government and its laws. As such, their protests do not really pose a threat to the Israeli apartheid; they act as if this discontent were an internal Jewish affair. In such conditions, a true act would be to propose a large democratic coalition that would include Palestinians. Such an act would be very risky, because it would break an unwritten rule of Israeli politics; however, only such a coalition, such a change in the coordinates of what appears to be possible, can prevent Israel from becoming just another religious fundamentalist racist state.

With all its horrors, the war in Ukraine offers another big opportunity. I fully support the basic stance of the German Green Party, which not only advocates full support for Ukraine but also proposes to use the ongoing oil and gas crisis as a unique chance to make our industries greener. The German Greens are thus travelling in a direction exactly opposite to the predominant Western politics, which keeps struggling with the problem of how to help Ukraine while limiting the impact of this 'help' on our established way of life. The Greens' plan is, rather, to use the Ukrainian war in a positive way: to view it not just as an obstacle but as an incentive for a general reorientation of our economy and social life. As Joseph Stiglitz put it:

it is a mistake to think that the war can be won with a peacetime economy. No country has ever prevailed in a serious war by leaving markets alone. Markets simply move too slowly for the kind of major structural changes that are required.[155]

This conclusion should be universalized: when confronted with new global crises, we will have to act fast, decisively and globally. Simon Jenkins's comment apropos the crisis in the UK's National Health Service is to be taken more literally than he perhaps meant it:

> This NHS crisis is historic – a war footing is the only way to deal with it. So we are left with today's emergency. Nothing diminishes the support and affection for frontline staff. Like soldiers in wartime, they are workers to whom people instinctively turn when all seems lost.[156]

The situation is similar across Europe, from Germany to my own Slovenia. To cope with our ongoing, escalating crises, from threats to our environment to unfolding wars, we will need elements of what, in this book, I provocatively call 'war Communism': mobilizations that will have to violate not only the usual market rules but also the established rules of democracy (enforcing measures and limiting freedoms without democratic approval)

A collection of Bertolt Brecht's (largely ignored or forgotten) short interviews and encounters was recently published under the title *Our Hope Today is the Crisis*.[157] Let's be courageous enough to fully endorse this insight: instead of just trying to escape, postpone, or minimize the threat posed by the four new riders of the apocalypse; instead of continuing to dwell in our melancholic apathy and frantically doing nothing, let's mobilize ourselves to attack the roots of our crisis, with all the risks that this involves. Because the greatest risk today is doing nothing and allowing history to follow its course.

Notes

1 Jean-Pierre Dupuy, *The War That Must Not Occur*, Redwood City: Stanford University Press, 2023 (quoted from the manuscript).

2 Jean-Pierre Dupuy, *Petite metaphysique des tsunamis*, Paris: Editions du Seuil, 2005, p. 19.

3 Ibid.

4 Dupuy, *The War That Must Not Occur*.

5 'Aliens haven't contacted Earth because there's no sign of intelligence here, new answer to the Fermi paradox suggests', *Live Science*, 15 December 2022: https://www.livescience.com/aliens-technological-signals.

6 See Thomas Frank: https://www.youtube.com/watch?v=VWKsTzHwIsM&t=2s

7 'Sanders warns Democrats not to focus solely on abortion ahead of midterms', *Guardian*, 10 October 2022: https://www.theguardian.com/us-news/2022/oct/10/bernie-sanders-democrats-warning-abortion-economy-midterms.

8 'Vladimir Putin fell down stairs at his home and soiled himself . . .', MailOnline, 2 December 2022: https://www.dailymail.co.uk/news/article-11494595/Vladimir-Putin-fell-stairs-home-soiled-himself.html.

9 '#PoopyPantsBiden: The REAL "accident" behind hashtag, and how trolls got it wrong', MEAWW.com, 8 November 2021: https://meaww.com/biden-bathroom-accident-happened.

10 'The disturbing secret behind the world's most expensive coffee', NationalGeographic.com: https://www.nationalgeographic.

com/animals/article/160429-kopi-luwak-captive-civet-coffee-Indonesia.

11 '"Forgetful Europe" urged to go through moral cleansing', BelTA, 2 July 2022: https://eng.belta.by/president/view/forgetful-europe-urged-to-go-through-moral-cleansing-151504-2022/.

12 Everyone should take a look at this horror: 'GOIDA! Russians advocate for dialogue and reason! Ivan Okhlobystin': https://www.youtube.com/watch?v=FMECmLXXPrs.

13 'Putin quoted song lyrics about rape and necrophilia to explain Russia's demands from Ukraine', BusinessInsider.com, 8 February 2022: https://www.businessinsider.com/putin-macron-meeting-quote-obscene-lyrics-show-russia-ukraine-demands-2022-2?r=US&IR=T

14 'Russia: Putin's statements on Chechnya may reflect public opinion', RadioFreeEurope/RadioLiberty, 13 November 2002: https://www.rferl.org/a/1101362.html.

15 Boris Čibej in *Delo* (Ljubljana), 14 February 2022.

16 Quoted from Moshe Lewin, *Lenin's Last Struggle*, Ann Arbor: University of Michigan Press, 2005, p. 61.

17 'The Russian spy boss humiliated by Putin', *El País*, 23 February 2022: https://english.elpais.com/opinion/2022-02-23/the-russian-spy-boss-humiliated-by-putin.html.

18 The scene is available at https://www.youtube.com/watch?v=09A-u8E0WcI.

19 Richard Overy, *The Dictators*, London: Penguin Books, 2004, pp. 100–101.

20 V. I. Lenin, 'The socialist revolution and the right of nations to self-determination', (January–February 1916): https://www.marxists.org/archive/lenin/works/1916/jan/x01.htm.

21 'Russia's Putin accused Lenin of ruining the Soviet Union', *Newsweek*, 22 January 2016: https://www.newsweek.com/russias-putin-accused-lenin-ruining-soviet-union-418519.

22 Leon Trotsky, *Problem of the Ukraine* (April 1939): https://www.marxists.org/archive/trotsky/1939/04/ukraine.html.

23 'Putin invokes Soviet heroes Lenin, Stalin, says Russia "created" Ukraine', *Newsweek*, 21 February 2022: https://www.newsweek.com/putin-invokes-soviet-heroes-lenin-stalin-says-russia-created-ukraine-1681185.

24 'China urges families to stock up on food for winter', *New York Times*, 2 November 2021: https://www.nytimes.com/2021/11/02/world/asia/china-food-shortages-winter.html.

25 'Time will prove China's stance on Ukraine is on the right side of history: Wang Yi', *Global Times*, 20 March 2022: https://www.globaltimes.cn/page/202203/1255298.shtml.

26 Alain Badiou, *Je vous sais si nombreux . . .*, Paris: Fayard, 2017, pp. 56–7.

27 'Étienne Balibar: "Le pacifisme n'est pas une option"', Mediapart, 7 March 2022: https://www.mediapart.fr/journal/culture-idees/070322/etienne-balibar-le-pacifisme-n-est-pas-une-option.

28 The poem can be heard at: https://knowyourmeme.com/memes/annalynne-mccord-dear-president-putin-im-so-sorry-i-was-not-your-mother.

29 As defined by Wikipedia: https://en.wikipedia.org/wiki/Realpolitik.

30 Quoted in 'Paris alive: Jean-Paul Sartre on World War II', *The Atlantic*, 3 September 2014: https://www.theatlantic.com/international/archive/2014/09/paris-alive-jean-paul-sartre-on-world-war-ii/379555/.

31 'Cryptocurrencies: anarchist turn or strengthening of surveillance capitalism?', *Australian Humanities Review* 66 (May 2020): https://australianhumanitiesreview.org/2020/05/31/cryptocurrencies-anarchist-turn-or-strengthening-of-surveillance-capitalism-from-bitcoin-to-libra/.

32 'Bosnian, US officials condemn Russian threat over Bosnia's Nato accession', *Intellinews*, 18 March 2022: https://www.intellinews.com/bosnian-us-officials-condemn-russian-threat-over-bosnia-s-nato-accession-238517/.

33 See https://asia.nikkei.com/Politics/International-relations/Russia-wants-NATO-forces-out-of-ex-Warsaw-Pact-states-Lavrov.

34 See Thomas Gomart and Nicholas Sowels, 'NATO-Russia: Is the "Russian Question" European?', *Politique étrangère*, vol. 5, 2009: https://www.cairn.info/revue-politique-etrangere-2009-5-page-123.htm.

35 See 'Medvedev: Russia may have to push back Poland's border for "peace"', *Daily Digest*: https://www.msn.com/en-gb/news/world/medvedev-russia-may-have-to-push-back-poland-s-border-for-peace/ss-AA184LyU?ocid=msedgntp&cvid=27d4ef23dc4f4631804eaaa74fe63db2&ei=11#image=2

36 Quoted from https://www.novilist.hr/novosti/zlokoban-intervju-utjecajnog-ruskog-politologa-europa-je-za-nas-trofej-koji-cemo-podijeliti-s-amerikancima/. Incidentally, this same Evstafiev said on Russia-1, a state-owned TV channel, that he supports public hanging of the Ukrainians condemned by a Russian court-martial for resisting the Russian peacekeeping mission – see 'Russian pundits advocate for public hangings in Ukraine on state-controlled TV', MirrorOnline, 14 March 2022: https://www.mirror.co.uk/news/world-news/russian-pundits-advocate-public-hangings-26463711

37 'Interview with Prime Minister Viktor Orbán in the political weekly *Mandiner*', *About Hungary*, 3 March 2022: https://abouthungary.hu/speeches-and-remarks/interview-with-prime-minister-viktor-orban-in-the-political-weekly-mandiner.

38 Franco Berardi, '*The Serpent's Egg*: between depression and aggressiveness', Medium.com: https://medium.com/neuromagma/the-serpents-egg-2367f08fecd1.

39 Moustafa Bayoumi, 'They are "civilised" and "look like us": the racist coverage of Ukraine', *Guardian*, 2 March 2022: https://www.theguardian.com/commentisfree/2022/mar/02/civilised-european-look-like-us-racist-coverage-ukraine.

40 'How One priest turned Putin's invasion into a Holy War', *Rolling Stone*, 19 March 2022: https://www.rollingstone.com/politics/politics-features/holy-war-priest-putin-war-ukraine-1323914/.

41 Quoted from Joanna Szostek on Twitter: https://twitter.com/Joanna_Szostek/status/1509258432863514634

42 Ibid.

43 'State channels prepare population for nuclear war – *The Moscow Times*', *Hindustan News Hub*: https://hindustannewshub.com/russia-ukraine-news/state-channels-prepare-population-for-nuclear-war-the-moscow-times/.

44 'Russia's military "is furious that Putin has down-scaled Ukraine invasion to focus on Donbas and is calling for all-out WAR'"', MailOnline, 27 April 2022: https://www.dailymail.co.uk/news/article-10759213/Are-fighting-war-masturbating-Russian-military-furious-Putin-scaled-invasion.html.

45 'Israel outrage at Sergei Lavrov's claim that Hitler was part Jewish', BBC News, 2 May 2022: https://www.bbc.co.uk/news/world-middle-east-61296682.

46 As set out in Mao's Three Worlds Theory, whereby the First World comprises the United States and the Soviet Union; the Second World comprises Japan, Canada, Europe and the other countries of the global North; and the Third World comprises China and India and the countries of Africa, Latin America and continental Asia.

47 See Frances Fukuyama, 'A country of their own: liberalism needs the nation', *Foreign Affairs*, May/June 2022: https://www.foreignaffairs.com/articles/ukraine/2022-04-01/francis-fukuyama-liberalism-country.

48 See 'Jürgen Habermas zur Ukraine: Krieg und Empörung', *Süd-deutsche Zeitung*, 28 April 2022: https://www.sueddeutsche.de/projekte/artikel/kultur/das-dilemma-des-westens-juergen-habermas-zum-krieg-in-der-ukraine-e068321/?reduced=true.

49 See 'What is the ne explétif and when to use it in French': https://french.kwiziq.com/revision/grammar/how-to-understand-the-ne-expletif.

50 I owe this idea to Eric Santner, Chicago (personal communication).

51 See 'Putin's "chef" who runs feared Wagner mercenaries calls the West "pathetic endangered perverts" . . .', MailOnline, 4 May 2022: https://www.dailymail.co.uk/news/article-10782799/Putins-chef-runs-feared-Wagner-mercenaries-calls-West-pathetic-endangered-perverts.html

52 See 'Why are UK supermarkets facing fresh food shortages?', *Guardian*, 22 February 2023: https://www.theguardian.com/business/2023/feb/22/problem-shortage-fresh-food-uk-supermarkets#:~:text=What%20is%20behind%20the%20shortages,energy%20bills%20to%20heat%20glasshouses.

53 I owe to Mladen Dolar this application of the 'four riders of the apocalypse' to today's condition.

54 See Trevor Hancock, 'There is a fifth horseman of the Apocalypse – and it is us', Healthy Debate, 5 November 2020: https://healthydebate.ca/2020/11/topic/there-is-a-fifth-horseman-humans/.

55 See 'War in Ukraine could lead to food riots in poor countries, warns WTO boss', *Guardian*, 24 March 2022: https://www.theguardian.com/world/2022/mar/24/war-ukraine-food-riots-poor-countries-wto-ngozi-okonjo-iweala-food-prices-hunger

56 'India and Pakistan heatwave is "testing the limits of human survivability," expert says,' CNN.com, 2 May 2022: https://

edition.cnn.com/2022/05/02/asia/india-pakistan-heatwave-climate-intl-hnk/index.html.

57 See https://en.wikipedia.org/wiki/Grass_Mud_Horse.

58 See https://www.youtube.com/watch?v=QkTZYjL_8f8.

59 'Medvedev raises spectre of Russian nuclear strike on Ukraine', Reuters, 27 September 2022: https://www.reuters.com/world/europe/russias-medvedev-warns-west-that-nuclear-threat-is-not-bluff-2022-09-27/.

60 'NATO would be too scared to react if Russia drops nuke first – Putin ally', *Newsweek*, 27 September 2022: https://www.newsweek.com/dmitry-medvedev-russia-nuclear-weapons-nato-ukraine-1746638.

61 'Restoration of empire is the endgame for Russia's Vladimir Putin', CNN.com, 11 June 2022: https://edition.cnn.com/2022/06/10/europe/russia-putin-empire-restoration-endgame-intl-cmd/index.html.

62 'U.S. needs strategic off-ramp to end Russian war in Ukraine', MSN.com:https://www.msn.com/en-gb/news/world/u-s-needs-strategic-off-ramp-to-end-russian-war-in-ukraine/ar-AA12kMOB?ocid=msedgntp&cvid=905166c2af0146a8bae52a8401544010.

63 Ibid.

64 'Restoration of empire is the endgame for Russia's Vladimir Putin', CNN.com, 11 June 2022: https://edition.cnn.com/2022/06/10/europe/russia-putin-empire-restoration-endgame-intl-cmd/index.html.

65 'Henry Kissinger, Noam Chomsky find rare common ground over Ukraine war', *Newsweek*, 24 May 2022: https://www.newsweek.com/henry-kissinger-noam-chomsky-find-rare-common-ground-over-ukraine-war-1709733.

66 See '"Freudian slip": Bush decries "invasion of Iraq" – not Ukraine', AlJazeera.com, 19 May 2022: https://www.aljazeera

.com / news / 2022 / 5 / 19 / freudian-slip-bush-decries-invasion-of-iraq-not-ukraine.

67 'Julian Assange can be extradited, says UK home secretary', BBC News, 17 June 2022: https://www.bbc.co.uk/news/uk-61839256.

68 See https://www.dw.com/en/us-intel-russia-war/a-61794064.

69 'Finland's leaders announce support for NATO membership, sparking retaliation threats from Russia', CNN.com, 13 May 2022: https://edition.cnn.com/2022/05/12/europe/finland-leaders-join-nato-intl/index.html.

70 'Dinner with the FT: Father to the oligarchs', *Financial Times*, 23 November 2004: https://www.ft.com/content/763b10fc-337e-11d9-b6c3-00000e2511c8.

71 ' "Insane" sanctions or food supplies: Russia tells West', *Hindustan Times*, 20 May 2022: https://www.hindustantimes.com/world-news/insane-sanctions-or-food-supplies-russia-tells-west-101652998007637.html.

72 'Grain initiative: rate of ship exits from ports remains critically low', *Hellenic Shipping News*, 1 February 2023: https://www.hellenicshippingnews.com/grain-initiative-rate-of-ship-exits-from-ports-remains-critically-low/.

73 'Russia's Sergei Lavrov compares Ukraine to Palestine', *Newsweek*, 16 May 2022: https://www.newsweek.com/russia-sergei-lavrov-compares-ukraine-palestine-putin-israel-1706810.

74 Ibid.

75 'China's Xi, in message to N.Korea's Kim, vows cooperation under "new situation" – KCNA', Reuters, 25 February 2022: https://www.yahoo.com/news/chinas-xi-message-n-koreas-221911185.html?guccounter=1.

76 ' "It's not rational": Putin's bizarre speech wrecks his once pragmatic image', *Guardian*, 25 February 2022: https://www.theguardian.com/world/2022/feb/25/its-not-rational-putins-bizarre-speech-wrecks-his-once-pragmatic-image.

77 'Putin's terrifying warning to the West', MailOnline, 24 February 2022: https://www.dailymail.co.uk/news/article-10545641/Putins-gives-chilling-warning-West-early-morning-TV-broadcast.html.

78 See 'An introduction to Ivan Ilyin', Open Culture: https://www.openculture.com/2018/06/an-introduction-to-ivan-ilyin.html.

79 'The Russians who fear a war with the West', BBC News, 25 October 2016: https://www.bbc.co.uk/news/world-europe-37766688.

80 'Trump calls Putin "genius" and "savvy" for Ukraine invasion', Politico, 23 February 2022: https://www.politico.com/news/2022/02/23/trump-putin-ukraine-invasion-00010923.

81 'Ukraine criticises speech by Pink Floyd's Roger Waters at UN Security Council', MSN.com: https://www.msn.com/en-gb/news/uknews/ukraine-criticises-speech-by-pink-floyd-s-roger-waters-at-un-security-council/ar-AA17goCj?ocid=msed gntp&cvid=c1b8dab2d9c64dc3a309f87d82bc86ef.

82 'Top Putin ally says he "will not hide" intention to invade Poland anymore', *Daily Beast*, 7 February 2023: https://www.thedaily-beast.com/top-putin-ally-ramzan-kadyrov-says-he-will-not-hide-intention-to-invade-poland-anymore.

83 Alenka Zupančič, *Let Them Rot: Antigone's Parallax*, New York: Fordham University Press, 2023, p. 18.

84 Quoted in 'Trump calls for the termination of the Constitution in Truth Social post', CNN.com, 4 December 2022: https://edition.cnn.com/2022/12/03/politics/trump-constitution-truth-social/index.html.

85 Quoted from 'Address by the President of the Federation', 21 February 2022: http://en.kremlin.ru/events/president/news/67828.

86 See https://www.youtube.com/watch?v=uyS1cXrsgIg.

87 Adam Tooze, *The Deluge*, London: Penguin Books, 2014, pp. 151–2.

88 Ibid., p. 166.

89 'Ukraine commits statue-cide', BBC News, 24 February 2014: https://www.bbc.co.uk/news/blogs-magazine-monitor-26321963.

90 Jean-Claude Milner, *Relire la Revolution*, Lagrasse: Verdier, 2016, p. 246.

91 See 'Vegetal redemption: a Ukrainian woman and Russian soldiers', The Philosophical Salon, 26 February 2022: https://thephilosophicalsalon.com/vegetal-redemption-a-ukrainian-woman-and-russian-soldiers/.

92 ' "Put sunflower seeds in your pockets so they grow on Ukraine soil when you DIE" ', MailOnline, 25 Febrary 2023: https://www.dailymail.co.uk/news/article-10548649/Put-sunflower-seeds-pockets-grow-Ukraine-soil-Woman-confronts-Russian-troops.html.

93 'Interview with Prime Minister Viktor Orbán in the political weekly *Mandiner*', *About Hungary*, 3 March 2022: https://about-hungary.hu/speeches-and-remarks/interview-with-prime-minister-viktor-orban-in-the-political-weekly-mandiner.

94 'Nori case: Bicocca, the course will be held – Icon News: https://www.ruetir.com/2022/03/02/nori-case-bicocca-the-course-will-be-held-icon-news/.

95 'Video shows sledgehammer execution of Russian mercenary', Reuters, 13 November 2022: https://www.reuters.com/world/europe/sledgehammer-execution-russian-mercenary-who-defected-ukraine-shown-video-2022-11-13/.

96 'Russia's Wagner Group sends bloodied sledgehammer to EU', *Daily Telegraph*, 24 November 2022: https://www.telegraph.co.uk/world-news/2022/11/24/putins-chef-wagner-group-sledgehammer-eu-response-called-terrorist/.

97 'Russia-Ukraine updates: EU agrees to cap Russian gas prices', AlJazeera.com, 2 December 2022: https://www.aljazeera.com/news/liveblog/2022/12/2/russia-ukraine-live-blog-shelling-in-kherson-leaves-three-dead.

98 'Putin's Private army goes full ISIS with sledgehammer execution video', Yahoo.com, 14 November 2022: https://www.yahoo.com/video/putin-private-army-goes-full-132201119.html.

99 'In Iran, young girls are forced to marry prison guards. Then executed the next day', Mamamia, 14 November 2022: https:/www.mamamia.com.au/iran-girls-execution/.

100 See Wikipedia: https://en.wikipedia.org/wiki/Itamar_Ben-Gvir.

101 'Netanyahu warns a "pernicious" form of antisemitism more popular today', Fox News, 12 November 2022: https://www.foxnews.com/world/netanyahu-warns-pernicious-form-antisemitism-popular-today.

102 'Netanyahu downplays right-wing anti-Semitism, contradicting Israeli study', *Times of Israel*, 27 January 2019: https://www.timesofisrael.com/netanyahu-downplays-right-wing-anti-semitism-contradicting-israeli-study/.

103 'Polish leader blames low birthrate on women using alcohol', Euronews, 8 November 2022: https://www.euronews.com/2022/11/08/polish-leader-blames-low-birthrate-on-women-using-alcohol.

104 'Gettysburg College postpones "Tired of white cis men?" event amid backlash', *Washington Examiner*, 14 November 2022: https://www.washingtonexaminer.com/restoring-america/equality-not-elitism/gettysburg-white-cis-men-backlash?utm_source=msn&utm_medium=referral&utm_campaign=msn_feed.

105 See https://framaforms.org/couloirs-en-mixite-choisie-16555 61648. I owe this information to Elias Cohen, ENS, Paris.

106 See 'University sparks language row as it advises students to refer to each other as "they"', MailOnline, 24 February 2023: https://www.dailymail.co.uk/news/article-11784439/Kent-University-sparks-woke-language-row-advice-refer-people-pronouns-unknown.html.

107 'Cambridge don in trans row after boycotting gender-critical speaker', *Daily Telegraph*, 21 October 2022: https://www.telegraph.co.uk/news/2022/10/21/cambridge-don-trans-row-boycotting-gender-critical-speaker/.

108 See 'Transgender rapist Isla Bryson moved to men's prison', BBC News, 26 January 2024: https://www.bbc.co.uk/news/uk-scotland-64413242.

109 'Muslim students from Goldsmiths University's Islamic Society "heckle and aggressively interrupt" Maryam Namazie talk', *Independent*, 4 December 2015: https://www.independent.co.uk/student/news/muslim-students-from-goldsmiths-university-s-islamic-society-heckle-and-aggressively-interrupt-maryam-namazie-talk-a6760306.html.

110 See 'Höcke schlägt Wagenknecht Wechsel in die AfD vor', Welt, 26 February 2023: https://www.welt.de/politik/deutschland/article243979899/Sahra-Wagenknecht-Hoecke-schlaegt-Wechsel-in-die-AfD-vor.html.

111 See John McWhorter, *Woke Racism: How a New Religion Has Betrayed Black America*, New York: Portfolio, 2021.

112 Vincent Lloyd, 'A Black professor trapped in anti-racist hell', *Compact*, 10 February 2023: https://compactmag.com/article/a-black-professor-trapped-in-anti-racist-hell.

113 I resume here the argumentation from Chapter 3 of my *Surplus-Enjoyment*, London: Bloomsbury Press, 2022.

114 Jacques Lacan, *The Four Fundamental Concepts of Psycho-Analysis*, Harmondsworth: Penguin Books, 1979, pp. 57–8.

115 Ben Brugis: *Canceling Comedians While the World Burns: A Critique of the Contemporary Left*, London: Zero Books, 2021.

116 Sama Naami, *Respektverweigerung: Warum wir fremde Kulturen nicht respektieren sollten. Und die eigene auch nicht*, Klagenfurt: Drava Verlag, 2015.

117 See Wikipedia: https://en.wikipedia.org/wiki/Lilla_Watson.

118 See 'Russia Vs. Ukraine or civil war In the West?': https://www.youtube.com/watch?v=JxdHm2dmvKE.

119 See 'Postmodernism is a transformation of Marxism': https://www.youtube.com/watch?v=oHu_RxxsoVA.

120 See 'An "imposter Christianity" is threatening American democracy', CNN.com, 24 July 2022: https://edition.cnn.com/2022/07/24/us/white-christian-nationalism-blake-cec/index.html.

121 'Viktor Orbán sparks outrage with attack on "race mixing" in Europe', *Guardian*, 24 July 2022: https://www.theguardian.com/world/2022/jul/24/viktor-orban-against-race-mixing-europe-hungary.

122 Ibid.

123 'GOP civil war on Ukraine builds between MAGA, Reagan Republicans', *The Hill*, 26 July 2022: https://news.yahoo.com/news/gop-civil-war-ukraine-builds-092040546.html.

124 Ibid. See also 'Rightwing Republicans rail against US aid for Ukraine: "We've done enough"', *Guardian*, 4 March 2023: https://www.theguardian.com/us-news/2023/mar/04/cpac-rightwing-republicans-ukraine-support-marjorie-taylor-greene.

125 Quoted from Chapter 1 of *The Communist Manifesto*: https://www.marxists.org/archive/marx/works/1848/communist-manifesto/ch01.htm.

126 'Judith Butler: "I am hopeful that the Russian army will lay down its arms"', *ARA*, 28 April 2022: https://en.ara.cat/culture/am-hopeful-that-the-russian-army-will-lay-down-its-arms_128_4353851.html

127 Simon Tisdall, 'Putin is already at war with Europe. There is only one way to stop him', *Guardian*, 17 July 2022: https://www.theguardian.com/commentisfree/2022/jul/17/putin-is-already-at-war-with-europe-there-is-only-one-way-to-stop-him.

128 'Volodymyr Zelensky and wife Olena: War is making our love stronger', *Daily Telegraph*, 27 July 2022: https://www.telegraph. co.uk/world-news/2022/07/27/volodymyr-zelensky-war-has-made-marriage-stronger/.

129 See James Godley, 'In the Shadow of Fire' (intervention at the conference *In the Wake of the Plague: Eros and Mourning* at Dartmouth College, 21–24 April 2022).

130 See Jacques Lacan, *Seminar VII :The Ethics of Psychoanalysis*, London: Routledge, 2015.

131 I rely here on Robert Pfaller, *Illusionen der Anderen*, Frankfurt: Suhrkamp, 2003.

132 Quoted from Adrian Johnston, 'Capitalism's Implants: A Hegelian Theory of Failed Revolutions', *Crisis & Critique*, 8, 2 (2021): https://www.crisiscritique.org/storage/app/media/2021-12-13/cc-82-adrian-johnston.pdf.

133 Étienne Balibar, *Spinoza and Politics*, New York: Verso, 1998, p. 88.

134 Christopher J. Bickerton and Carlo Invernizzi Accetti, *Technopopulism: The New Logic of Democratic Politics*, Oxford: Oxford University Press, 2021, p. 7.

135 See 'How Prince Harry makes his millions – inside Duke and Duchess of Sussex £135m empire', *Daily Express*: https://www.msn.com/en-gb/money/other/how-prince-harry-makes-his-millions-inside-duke-and-duchess-of-sussex-135m-empire/ar-AA16yAcx?ocid=msedgntp&cvid=d7e7bc8c98974846b92872c7b0937c7.

136 '2% of Elon Musk's wealth could help solve world hunger, says director of UN food scarcity organization, CNN.com, 1 November 2021: https://edition.cnn.com/2021/10/26/economy/musk-world-hunger-wfp-intl/index.html

137 See 'The market is not an end in itself', *Financial Times*, 16 September 2022: https://www.ft.com/content/0affdc86-0148-4d1e-80f3-4b7e0d2d5bc2.

138 'Hatte Marx doch recht?', *Der Spiegel*, 30 December 2022: https://www.spiegel.de/wirtschaft/gruener-kapitalismus-die-chance-auf-eine-nachhaltigere-wirtschaftsordnung-a-00f49cb5-6509-456f-94ad-f420fab94200.

139 Marx and Engels, *Collected Works*, vol. 47, Moscow: Progress Publishers, 1995, p. 234.

140 V. I. Lenin, 'People From Another World', from *Collected Works*, vol. 26, Moscow: Progress Publishers, Moscow, 1972, pp. 431–3: https://www.marxists.org/archive/lenin/works/1918/jan/06.htm.

141 See Roland Boer, *Socialism with Chinese Characteristics: A Guide for Foreigners*, Singapore: Springer, 2021. The book is dedicated to Domenico Losurdo, who wrote *Stalin: The History and Critique of a Black Legend* (available online at https://static1.squarespace.com/static/5ed33bcd368e221ec227cacd/t/5ee39a1731781f54f197c5f7/1591974443348/Domenico+Losurdo+-+Stalin.pdf); like Losurdo, Boer treats Stalin as one of the big names in the Marxist revolutionary tradition.

142 See Søren Mau, *Mute Compulsion*, London: Verso Books, 2023.

143 Marx and Engels, *Collected Works*, vol. 24, Moscow: Progress Publishers, 1989. p. 183.

144 See George Orwell, *The Road to Wigan Pier* (1937).

145 Quoted from Johnston, 'Capitalism's Implants'.

146 See, for example, 'Inside the strange, paranoid world of Julian Assange', Buzzfeed.com, 23 October 2016: https://www.buzzfeed.com/jamesball/heres-what-i-learned-about-julian-assange.

147 See, for example, 'Is WikiLeaks founder being granted freedom because of bad hygiene?' Yahoo.com, 13 January 2018: https://www.yahoo.com/lifestyle/wikileaks-founder-granted-freedom-bad-hygiene-213048566.html.

148 See, for example, 'Whistleblower Julian Assange sounds off on #MeToo Twitter campaign', *Newsweek*, 23 October 2017: https://

www.newsweek.com/julian-assange-sounds-me-too-campaign-690950.

149 Alenka Zupančič, 'When I count to ten, you will be dead . . .', *Mladina-Alternative*, Ljubljana, 2013, p. 31.

150 'Facebook whistleblower Frances Haugen calls for urgent external regulation', *Guardian*, 25 October 2021: https://www.theguardian.com/technology/2021/oct/25/facebook-whistleblower-frances-haugen-calls-for-urgent-external-regulation.

151 See 'What Zuckerberg's metaverse means to our humanity', CNN.com, 29 October 2021:https://edition.cnn.com/2021/10/28/opinions/zuckerberg-facebook-meta-rushkoff/index.html.

152 'We have strikes, protests and scandals – Ukraine is more than a warzone', *Guardian*, 22 February 2023: https://www.theguardian.com/commentisfree/2023/feb/22/strikes-protests-scandals-ukraine-warzone.

153 'Israel is annexing the West Bank. Don't be misled by its gaslighting', *Just Security*, 9 February 2023: https://www.justsecurity.org/85093/israel-is-annexing-the-west-bank-dont-be-misled-by-its-gaslighting/

154 Ibid.

155 Joseph Stiglitz, 'Wars aren't won with peacetime economies', *Project Syndicate*, 17 October 2022: https://www.project-syndicate.org/commentary/west-needs-war-economics-energy-food-supply-shortages-by-joseph-e-stiglitz-2022-10.

156 Simon Jenkins, 'This NHS crisis is historic – a war footing is the only way to deal with it', *Guardian*, 2 January 2023: https://www.theguardian.com/commentisfree/2023/jan/02/britain-nhs-crisis-war-footing-pandemic.

157 See Bertolt Brecht, *Unsere Hoffnung heute ist die Krise,* ed. Von Noah Willumsen, Frankfurt: Suhrkamp Verlag, 2023.